UNDER VIRGA

Joe Amato

CHAX PRESS 2006

Front cover art by Maria Tomasula: *All I Know*, copyright ©2000 by the artist.

Back cover: Penfield Manufacturing Co., Syracuse, New York, with shell of
Victorian house at top. Photo taken by author April 1990. Mattress factory
founded 1892, closed December 2005.

A portion of this book was published earlier in *EOAGH,* to which grateful
acknowlegement is made. See www.chax.org/eoagh.

Printed in the USA

Published by Chax Press.
101 West Sixth Street
Tucson, Arizona 85701-1000
USA

ISBN 0-925904-56-2

for the hell of it

& for Kass Fleisher

That's why I can't ever be a preacher again. Preacher's gotta know.
I don't know. I gotta ask.

> John Carradine as Casy
> in John Ford's *The Grapes of Wrath*

The day will come when we will have to know
the answers.

> Diane di Prima, *Revolutionary Letters*

Alpha

<u>The Way In Is Never Satisfactory</u>

"You made it"

to the end of your worries

"Say, what's a girl like you"
like?

You made it

to the end of your worries.

You made it, Ginger, and you
too, Señor Gaspar.

Was it new? Well—
kinda. At least you
made it, got it
made, kinda: a name
for yourself. And it was real
most of it, researched.
The research one does.
For a movie
without a storyline. Or punch
line. As such. But slug lines
aplenty. Isn't that
so, Stanislavsky?

Your attention, please:

Now what. Simply that
writing can be about one's inner
demons, sure. Or finding
oneself. Or actually caring
about something
that actually happens
to someone else. In a hard
luck world. But to communicate
that and little else
as we delve deeper
into who we are, we once

were. Would this be
tantamount to success, this writing ex
post facto thing. Or is it bringing us u-t-d
with contemporary institutional survival
skills. Or is it mere moment
by moment
vanity on both
our parts.

And how might attention span
facticities of the sort found
here, on the line, or
Cc line, amid or
among voices (note the
plurals). I'm not afraid you'll
see right
through me. Like any number
of former students. It's OK, and
thank you too.

Further, you put the stuff in last
advises Marcella
that gives off
the most liquid. (I'll skip the two
Italian terms.) You need
a hot pan, she insists, or hot enough
to do some damage. This allows a "layering"
of flavors, each subsequent ingredient
picking up the flavor
of the ingredient prior.

See the Aug./Sept. 2004 issue of *Saveur*.

It's as good a method as any
if you're to have anything at all to do
with taste
or method.

[Pause.]

"As casualties rise
he fires back at his critics."
These dead metaphors
can kill you
more quicky than an excess of stuntmen

or digital effects artists.

[Rewind. I can't give you the soundtrack
for your life. That
you'll have to determine
on your own.]

For starters, then, which can be rough-
going, esp. if you're predisposed
to rather precise registers
of mood, we find we must
Report Suspicious Activities
(1-800-492-TIPS), esp. in the vicinity
of the accidentally
on purpose. Oh &

WARNING—SPOILERS AHEAD!

The quest for meaning
one surmises, meaning
one drops a dime on anything
that doesn't smell like Poetry
with a capital Y.

[Drop that dime, soldier!]

To which the only rational response is
"The butler did it."

Let the record show, then, that
the butler did it.

And let us continue
to provide some semblance
of continuity
before the stage
pulls into Lordsburg, pards: the difficulty obtains
not in knowing
how to ask
but in knowing how to ask
how to know
while entertaining the possibility
of entertainment. To be a preacher
and not, in conclusion, the new duck
& cover routine alone

bidding us continue
to provide etc.

Don't shoot
the decoys!

Whence memory operates
under the gravity of small moons, always
under the table

                (i.e., self-regulated compensation
                for the examined life)

under the weather

                (i.e., dues paid
                and no medical benefits to speak of)

under virga

                (i.e., if you look it up you'll find
                that it never hits the ground)

                (i.e., the grounded).

Recall: how can you be so
singular, she sd to him, so
ringed.

(Cont'd)

Bravo

It can be a bitch, OK? Under the spell
of poetry, writing
language, trope, narrative, book, concept
feeling, pink
slip, box
office, thought
slipping a bit, I'd write

"the whole freakin' shebang"

whittled down
to worry one man's solitary
                              (i.e., if we can yet speak
                              of the solitary)
what
yearnings?

"I shit you not."

So it's a joke, a freakin'
fuckin' joke
most of the time, us
and our little, what—
did you say *books*?

More whittlings, piling up
these days at the rate of
two+ billion a year, or
like never before, as I read
online, in a book, books
snapped up like hamburgs, whittled
like nibs.
          (in that they lead, you see
          to more books.

          It will behoove us
          to have an eye throughout
          for hunger.)

"And so," he explained
squatting bare-assed
over a small mirror, "this way

I can excavate my asshole
to find some really big
words." Thus posed, then
the problem became one
of how big an asshole
was required
to render unto Caesar
the things that nobody
not even Caesar, bless him
cared to hear. (At an earlier mirror
stage, I alleged
of myself, "I'm twice
the poet that you are." "Uh-huh"
I hastened to reply.) Which is
to say—but aposiopesis
brings us hither
and takes us yon
and it is to yon
that we must now repair
having drawn dangerously close
to the sobriety of
that restrictive clause
hither, to do unto
otters…

No need to fret then, no, but whither
shall we go
with all that meat
& no p'tatuz? At any rate, please

STOP WRITING

"—*unless your words are a way to a better life.®*"

Charlie

Delta

Bravo, Charlie!

If I were an optimist
and I am
I'd tell you about the time
on your hands, how little of it
is available 12345
for trifling matters 54321.
                              (watch that pinkie
                              Victor Charlie)

Wait—I've already suggested as much.

On to something more
specific, more
epic, or
ETHNIC   (GOOD
                              THRU 12/02)

Echo

The trick is to keep the reader reading, you see.

Everything else rides on this trick, captured
imaginations aside.

"But what do you mean by
reading, bespectacled
man?" The answer will have something
to do with writing, and which bugs
to bear must be
borne, and which swept
under the rug, and which
debugged, with reckless
abandon, to yield the absolute
zero of predicament.

Blah blah blah
the alphabet you have
blah blah blah
not the alphabet you wish you had?

Yo, Vinny—yo real ain't worth dick maybe, but
the trick is to keep the reader reading, you see
twiddle-dee-dee.

Foxtrot

"Am I?"

So there I was, as I say
under virga. There
we were. And it occurs to me just now
that I wanted this to be my "America [West]
poem"—the poem all
                              (i.e., most)
US poets
feel compelled to write
sooner than later, but sooner
or later
much as other American poets
                              (there and
                              hither
                              and yon).

Can such a thing be writ
in such an age? Not exceptionalism, no
or brinkmanship, more like
specificity:

          Lafayette, CO 80026
          Normal, IL 61761
          N. Syracuse, NY 13212
          The North Side
          of Syracuse, NY _____

Borders but the membrane
of the global:

          The Americas.
                              (as above
                              partaking)

Still, ought such a thing
to be writ, ought re[**]gion
to be so regionalized, regionalized
so? And does "radical social artifice"
                              (where have I read that?
                              it gives me goosebumps
                              when accompanied by

                              cream of wheat)
mean that somebody
is putting somebody else on
notice, and that this will have
the net effect
of delivering both parties unto
their roots
par avion?

Or ought that line
                          (i.e., the American
                          unum)
that lineage
to be broken once
and for all, out of one
the all?

"Can you, huh? Can you really?"

and

"Where's Chuck Jones
when you need him?"

and

"Did you know *hot key*
is now a dictionary entry
and has been for two decades?"

and

"I guess that's a Great
Lake over there, but Jesus
Christ, which one?"

and

"How many shower curtain
rods is one expected to consume
over the course of one's life?"

and

"You mean you like blacks

but not African Americans,
is that it?"

Me, a little 7:30, I've found that
I'm more comfortable here
than elsewhere—*here*
without footnotes, lacking
the patience, I suppose it is
for such, what
standards? Though I do love
standards, thou witty. And what means it
to be more comfortable *here*?
      "to be more *comfortable* here"?
in front of my machine
    "*my* machine"?
peering out the window
and up our street
    "*our* street"?
longing for a different vista
a different ethnic vista, even
      who am I kidding?
preoccupied with another occupation
     sort of
if territorially no less Gertrude-ish
or Stein-ish.

Let's not get too ethical or
experimental about it, one
too many pros-
theses hurled into the air
of pure conjecture.

But *is* clarity required
to grasp these opacities
of place
and affect
and placement?

"You mean, the eternal verities
one reads about
every Sunday
morning in the *NYTBR*?"

"You mean, defenestration?"

"You mean, peace be upon you
a Fardh Prayer?"

I mean "Purple Haze"
fella, or anywhere
where the deep purple
falls across the garden
of experience. America
as a rave? Or Texas
Hold'em, with a little X
on hand? All long after
my time, folks
                              (e.g., "Blow me
                              dude").
Come to think of it
I could use some
head just about now.

Honey?

These kids today, yknow
are like us in some ways, but
come equipped with much higher quality
taboos.
                    (Me, I wouldn't even pierce
                    an ear.)

For "clarity"
                    (as above)
substitute "elasticity," and reread. Your answers
will be recorded
for posterity
in the annals of dance
or the plastic arts. And please recall that
emotional truths, like
trim, while vitally important
are as accessible
as a rainy day, even a bleach-bypassed
rainy day. You can fake a rainy day, that is
but not an emotional truth, as even [male] blobs
in suits or any student
acting the part
of student
will tell you.

And so I've learned to trust the seasons
but what to do
about the reasons?

To live longer, when you get
right down to it, might settle
the matter.   Long
enough, she sd meantime, thus documenting
a preference.

Golf

FUCK GOLF
part of me wants to say.

It's a class thing, that part
of me.

                              Subject: Please Confirm Your Identity

The other part
wants me to admire
the unencumbered walk, the steady swing
through today's manicured territories, baby
that perforce require a ton of water
and chemicals, the destruction
of global habitat and, to date
myself, an old crooner
selling orange juice. Fuckitall, I need
to relax? in the face of such
impurities?

This, therefore, will not have been
my "America [West] poem."

"You're just not up to it?
Even up there, looking
down?"

Roger that.

Hotel

But I hasten to add
that America, its landscape of Super
8's or some aspect of it
as ~~once~~ I once knew it
and as I am coming to know it a-
new, at once courtesy of

(   )

and

(heartbreak
hotel of course)

will play a key role here
and not merely as the prevailing planetary source
of neoliberal possibility and
crazy privatized woe.

My wife Kass

(I have a wife
named Kass
who fancies herself something of an economist
of sorts
and a wife)

interjects, accordingly, over the din
of bad classic rock
I subject myself to daily
to atone for the lip
service I pay
to the simpler life
I once enjoyed ~~once~~:

"Will the mass luxury market create good jobs
for the many
as some are claiming
it will do, and will it do
so without meanwhile
for instance
destroying the planet?"

(I am paraphrasing
reception fuzzy)

We both sip our Starbucks decaf house blend
(she takes Splenda)
our brows deeply furrowed

as we brainstorm, develop
a plan to enter
the fourth quintile, a place
we, or at least I
imagine
of duty-free collaboration
and superb cheeses.

(She really does.)

India

I know.

"Is this what you call poetry?"

Very well then. Please consider this item
a letter of application. Or a job
talk.

I would like a better job, more
respect, a new stainless
steel
stove.

As a letter of application
or a job talk

>   (and should you find academic pain
>   moot, please feel free to
>   skip ahead
>   or zone out)

it bears witness
to its generative conditions.

Everywhere you look it says
"Hire me."

Everywhere you look it says
"Outsource *this*
motherfucker."

Everywhere you look
the problem of representation
or its absence.

"I need an agent
or agency."

To which:

Please wait while we find an Agent to assist you...
All Agents are currently busy. Please stand by.
An Agent will be with you in a moment. Thank you for your patience.
The next available Agent will be with you in a moment.

Currently experiencing network delays, one moment please....
Network connection re-established.
All Agents are currently busy. Please stand by.
An Agent will be with you in a moment. Thank you for your patience.
The next available Agent will be with you in a moment.
All Agents are currently busy. Please stand by.
An Agent will be with you in a moment. Thank you for your patience.
The next available Agent will be with you in a moment.
You have been connected to Oliver Twist.

Sadly, poor Oliver was not much help.

Up next, courtesy of the beloved
MLA Job Information List:

The intent of this description is to illustrate the types of duties & responsibilities that will
be required of positions given this title & should not be interpreted to describe all the specific
duties & responsibilities that may be required in any particular position. Directly related
education/experience beyond the minimum stated may be substituted where appropriate
at the discretion of the Appointing Authority.

What can one say? Fuckin'
pain in the ass PLUS

which is to say, prose is not
out of the question, not
for me, bud. And I didn't say, either
that I want to bury
my cock
up some reader's or
Appointing Authority's
ass. And I didn't
not say. And shouldn't that be
indie? Gotta go, my wings
are burning.

                    Respectfully submitted,

Juliet

But first: call a dandelion
a weed
or a flower, a dandelion
is a dandelion, not a cell
phone. A poem is neither a cell
nor a phone
optimally, but a poem
comprises word-things
the thingness of which
does not foreclose
on conceptual mobility
the way other species
of thingnesses
might. Does
this word-thing
some prefer to call
                (for lack of a better word
                -thing)
a poem
hit you in the solar
plexus? If not, perhaps
I've phoned it
in.

OK:

A poem is music.

"But what if you can't hear?"

A poem is vision.

"But what if you can't see?"

A poem is feeling.

"But what if you can't feel?"

If you can feel, you can see.

If you can feel, you can hear.

If you can think, you can figure out
the orchestration.

AN ADVANTAGE!
                        (extremely rare in these climes)

If you can't feel
If you can't feel

the structure, structures, strictures
                        (comes cheap)
heaping up
over, comprising

and there is a pronounced dislike, too

"I dislike sloppy translation
passing for transcontinental or
cosmopolitan
                        (ca. 1798)
creds"

one among many
popular career credos, I am led by the evidence
                        (*coming soon!*)
to believe, that would forgo
the real work of meaning, ergo
we have a hankering for
a literate world
absent those "real deals"
who
                                                            sour grapes
                                        and the infrequent genius aside

aspire to bore us all shitless, it would seem
with their fastidiously configured
sentences, paragraphs, lines and
hairdos.

STOP WRITING

"If you wear shitkickers
does that make you a shitkicker?"

Yes, I believe
it do, and that's the best
I can do.

Kilo

I'm ad-libbing, of course. Retyping too quickly
                              (i.e., as measured in nautical
                              miles per hour)
yields "mad-libbing." Huh. Anyway. Remember
when *touchy-feely*
came into vogue?

What a year.

Hence,

"Guilty as charged."

The dog chewed my leather laces, that little fucker
when I asked, naively
whether we need more men
who act like women
or more women
who act like men. Sorry but
contrition is not my strong suit
esp. when I'm high
on banana peels.

Lima

Let's get down to brass tacks, soldier:

first, *brass* is an alloy chiefly of copper and zinc
"in variable proportions"
according to my red, white & blue
                         (and orange)
dictionary, 11th ed.

The word itself evidently
goes back to a Middle English word, *bras*
meaning, in middle America
and Peru, simply
"metal."
                         (so much
                         so good)

All of which means
I did doctoral work in English, or
Give Me Props.

You will find none of that
here—brass, that is—whether utensils, empty
cartridges, tablets, bushings
or tacks.

But careful readers will be sure to note
gall, horns
                         (you may toss your salt
                         behind thee)
and the occasional high-ranking government official.

Also, that some asses
may not be flattered
by capri pants.

One aim would be
to try to figure out
what's worth saying
and what's not, hi-ho
hi-ho.

Oh & that word, "chiefly," may require some elaboration
upon revision.

Mike

9 December 2002

Mike,

The tale hangs hence, where it picks up an additional
context, an outside
"inside" another flatulent "volume"
                   (see *Finger Exorcised*)
but therein absent
                   (listed, technically, and listing
                   but without enlisting
                   21 lists)
and herein in 10 pt font
                   (mostly)
to reduce whittling
                   (among other things)
and drive my publisher
                   (a gentle soul
                   whom I enjoy ribbing
                   and driving)
bonkers, to wit:

26252423

22

Authors Anonymous, Inc. , Zhang Ymou
Voters for a Transgenic Nomenclature
The Lollipop Guild
Burson-Marsteller (Poetry Division)
Random House Trade Publishing Group
The House of the Rising Sun
Animal House
Barnes & Noble
AWP
MLA, MLM, M & M, AFI, DEA, Twiggy, Danny Aiello, Aibo Pet, Pet Rock, House on the Rock
NCTE, Hakim Bey, Peter Lamborn Wilson, Edward Teach, The Oregon Trail, Chimney Rock, the ymir
AAUP, Rock of Ages, the radical center, Mocambo, Mel's drive-in
SAWSJ
SLS
ASME
ISA
SPD, SPT
E(lectronic)L(iterature)O(rganization), *EJOURNAL*, EFF, C. H. Knoblauch, Ronald Bosco, Helen Elam
Illegal Aliens, Resident Aliens, Brian Lamb, studs, bombshells, Destry, Marlene Dietrich, tinhorns
The Foreign Legion, American Legion, British Board of Film Censors, American Plastics Council
The Foreign Office, all-Americans
Office of Homeland Security, Biotic Baking Brigade, Salma Hayek, Friedrich Hayek, Janet Lyon
Foreigner, Foreigners, Jabès, Erich Auerbach Erich Auerbach, Madam Librarian, Adonis, Cixous, Jacques
WASPS, men of letters, men of action, San Quentin, DSL, Kelly Munson
Women of Color, Women's Bean Project, Larry Talbot, Maria Ouspenskaya, Mercury Theater
He-men, Miss America, Miss World, Miss Universe, MI-6, Ecomcon, Official Verse Cult
ure, Sissies, Nerds, Crackpots, Addicts, Hacks, Hackers, scabs, phonies, The Yes Men, Miss Piggy, Trolls
Everyone Behind The Curtain, Addison DeWitt, Boy George, OTB, non-ladder faculty, ambulance chasers
Miller Brewing Co.
Bristol-Myers Co., Bristol-Myers Squibb
Molson (Golden)
Benbow Chemical
M & M Ponto's Produce
The Crocodile Hunter
Mick Dundee, Hunter Gray
Carrier Corporation (United Technologies), CCCS, CYA, free spirits, wedded souls, Bear River
Lon Chaney, Jr.
Hyde Park (Chicago) and the Parrots of Hyde Park (Chicago), South Park, The South, Never Never Land
Jesus Christ
The Man Who Knew Too Much
Ian Gillan, Gilbert & Sullivan, Volunteer, Lace, Damian Judge Rollison, Maureen Seaton, Nuremberg
Murray Head, Edith Head, Ray Charles, Sarah Fisher, Peter Pan, Angela Lansbury, Toots Thielemans
Judas Iscariot, Pandora, Frank Wedenkind, absentminded professors, Jamie Foxx, The Mick, Jack Kilby

Peter Lorre, Jeannie (dreamt of), Movie Loft, Cokie Roberts, Samson, Jean Cocteau, Alexis de Tocqueville
Number One Son ("We shall now have tea/and speak of absurdities"), The Cocoanut Grove, Karl Rove
Madonna, Vito Corleone, The Redgraves, Donnie Darko, Xlibris, The Molly Gibson, Frances McDormand
Taurus Car Club of America, La Femme Nikita (ca. 1990), George Will, Red Barber, Eminem, Ron Popeil
Pi Mu Epsilon, Pi Tau Sigma National Honarary Mechanical Engineering Fraternity, M Street, Judah
Syracuse University, Académie française, Sun Tzu, Fido, Stephen Crane, Aaron Sorkin, The Iozia Family
Jack Spicer, you cocksucker you
Rimbaud, Jack Napis, Jack-in-the-box, Jack Frost, Jack-of-all-trades, Crackerjack, Jack Greene & Lisa Trank,
Ralph & Norton, The Vatican, Max Bialystock, Max Bickford, MaxPaul, Max Headroom, Simone
Signoret, Frank Borzage, The Flash, Tony Robbins, Joe Bananas, Joe the Bartender, David Barsamian
Kevin, owner of Joe's Italian Kitchen (Louisville, CO), Tony Blair, David Blair, Victor Moore, Bob Dorian
La Familia (Lafayette, CO), The Friedmans, Bob Andrews, Bob Costas, Benjamin Netanyahu, Benji, Joe
Camel, Ricky Skaggs, *How Not To Do It Yourself* (15th ed.), La Mexicana (Bridgeport, Chicago), Siam, Tulsa,
Flatt & Scruggs, Crockett & Tubbs, H. Ross Perot, Davy, Davy Crockett, Rocket Man, Simon, Paul Krugman,
Ezra Pound, Fluxus, Phaedrus, Coyote, Beep Beep, Spinal Tap, Che, Fidel, Carmen, Benny

21
Binion, da kine, ERA, The Robb Report, Lewis Black, Shiprock, producers, Man of a Thousand Faces
The USA I Saw In My Chevrolets, *The Protocols of the Elders of Zion*
——The Mason-Dixon——The Maginot Line——Magna Carta, Bill of Rights, The Ides of March, BITNET
Warner Oland, Pop Warner, Jane Pauley, *Jane's*, Khyber Pass, street people, pickpockets, Chicken Little
Nigel Bruce, Daryl Zero, Dixie, 5th Column, The Conch Republic, Fairview USA, Verlaine, Max Adams
Sherlock, Jr., Bennett Cerf, Damon Runyon, Ada1852, Jeff Greenfield, William Bennett, George F. Will
The Saint, Khrushchev, H. R. Giger, Ridley Scott, Charlie Daniels, The Next Big Thing, The Piltdown Man
George Soros, Jeff Bezos, Bill Gates, Tom Terrific, Prince Valiant, Henry Louis Gates Jr., Hannah Crafts
The Thin Man
Phi Beta Kappa, Charles Babbage, Augusta Ada Byron, beta versions, The Fugitive, D.J.'s, ringtone D.J.'s
The Knights of Pythias, The Central School of Speech and Drama, The New School, The Old School
NPR, Nadezhda Konstantinovna Krupskaya, USSR, ordinary Joes, Popeye, Popeye Doyle, Gene Autry
NRA
NBC (GE)
ABC
CBS, BC, BCE, AD, Neptune Mountaineering, Jean Baudrillard, Gelatin, Marina Abramovic
USA, PTA, PTSD, SPCA, ILWU, The Hardy Boys, James Byrd Jr., James Meredith, Nancy Drew, TCP/IP
AMC (+), XTC, FOB, SSL, ISBN, Library of Congress, DARPA, Tom Petty, John Mellencamp, The Big O
Bravo, Robert Byrd, Larry Bird, John Doerr, Maryanne Del Gigante, Charlea Rorick, The Jolly Green Giant
Communications Code, VSOP, Pavlov, this little piggy, Masters of the Universe, squares, Mummers
The Self, BBC, Paul Laurence Dunbar, William Dean Howells, The Tokugawa Family, Johannes Gutenberg
Operation Desert Storm, Operation Infinite Justice, Operation Enduring Freedom, Operation Overlord
Operation TIPS, Al Jazeera, The Situationists, the Soixante-Huitards, William Gates Sr., Andrew Carnegie
Lord Pretender, Pretenders, The Wealth of Nations [w/o emphasis], George Clooney, MPAA, Lenin
Amato Opera, Samuel Alito, Anton "Nino" Scalia, John Cassavetes, Terrence Howard
Amato Food|Fuel, John Sweeney, The Red Cross, AP, UPI, Westworld, Tinsel Town
Richard Burton, Robert Rich, Tim Burton, William Cameron Menzies, Lawrence Livermore National Lab

Leonard Peltier Defense Committee, World Bank, Burning Man, Tom Bopp, Eleanor Roosevelt
Lawrence Welk, Leo Ornstein, Juxtapostional Knighthood, Inc., Owsley Stanley, Ernst Neizvestny
Jay Silverheels, Tom Mix, Midnight Cowboy, Sagwitch, Singin' Sandy, The Chippendales, The Desert Fox
Christopher Columbus, cris cheek, Chris Mazura, All My Children, The Men Who Would Be Kipling
Kemo Sabe, Goldfinger, Lotte Lenya, Côte d'Azur, David Baptiste Chirot, Laura Kightlinger, Sir Gawain
The Man, GOP, The Confidence Man, the pickup man, Ty Murray, Dasher Dancer etc., Leonard Skinner
Mr. Clean, Mr. Ed, Criswell, Stan & Olly, Edgar G. Ulmer, CPR, Andrew Sarris, King Tut, Ry Cooder
Stanley Steemer, Carpet Cleaner, B. F. Skinner, The Vanishing Voter Project, "Fatty" Sakall, Jean Rouch
NARAL, 750/4, Anne Landers, Robin Leach, Béla Bartók, Béla Balázs, Rudolf Arnheim, Steve Biko
University of Illinois at Chicago, The Ziegfeld Girls, John Chancellor, Jim Lehrer, [Goodbye] Mr. Chips, John
Walsh, Bob & Ray, 1-800-FARM-AID, Mr. T, Cuban crocodiles, Stanley Lieber, pinup girls
Route 66 (Alternate Route: where you got *your* kicks), GRE, SAT, The Iowa Test, 77 Sunset Strip, PhD, pH
Taxi (when I'm stoned), Sonar Tax Law, 4th Estate, The Sullivan Bros., Sky Chefs, Ride, Sally Ride
Casey Jones, Carolyn Jones, Gomez, Herman Munster, The Great Stone Face, MIB, The Human Cairn
The Road to Zanzibar, HAL, IBM, the transcendental signified, Judith Johnson
The Road to Kandahar, The Road to Utopia, Gus Arnheim and his Ambassadors, Chef Boy-R-D
Mt. Audubon, merrily merrily merrily merrily, ACT, LSAT, GMAT, MD, DDS, JD, PE, NFG, BA, BS, MA
The Empire State, WTC, The Hancock Building, The Drake, Grand Hotel, The Keystone State, The Fort
Garry, The Eiffel Tower, The City by the Bay, City of Lights, Panama City, Panama Canal Zone, Panama Red,
Erie Canal, The City That Never Sleeps, The City That Works, Double Happiness, Luckenbach, Texas, Paris,
Texas, The Lark Tavern, Salt City, Thomas Wolfe, The Marketplace of Ideas (resized)
University at Albany
Cazenovia College, The Boys from Syracuse, Ellen DeGeneres, Rosie, Roy Jones Jr., Thom Swiss
Brian Eno, Philip Glass, Ludwig Mies van der Rohe, László Moholy-Nagy, The Windsors, Robert Ludlum
London, Michaelmas Term lately over, David Copperfield, David Blaine, Laird Hamilton, SAE, FUBAR
University of Illinois at Urbana-Champaign, Steve Dorner, Douglas Brode, Ratso Rizzo, the exurbs
Wayne's World, UbuWeb, The Orange, The Nittany Lions, SAG, squeegee man, public intellectuals
WGA, First Motion Picture Unit, the right of way, Ravi Shankar, The Newsbreakers, crumpers
NWU, CPI, FOD, mph
NOW
ACLU, JAMA, STD, ESL, ASL, ACL, Helen Keller, Anne Sullivan, Anne Bancroft, W. E. B. DuBois
The Foresight Institute, The "We shall yammer yammer yammer as you stammer stammer stammer" Club

20
Illinois Institute of Technology
The Planetary Society, MexicanPerforation, Indian Larry, Billy Lane, Injun Joe, Ohio, Harold Prince
Planet of the Apes, Howard Prince, Garrison Keillor, Lillian Virginia Mountweazel, Prince Charming
The Faculty of the University of Colorado at Boulder, Lunar Society of Birmingham, The Rijkswaterstaat
The Nutty Professor (ca. 1963), Shukojuku (Emperor Protection Corps), Champion, Trigger, San Marino
Dobie Gillis, Gil Scott-Heron, Kojak, Blofeld, John Dudgeon, knight bachelor
Maynard G. Krebs, The Red Army, Smersh, The Equalizer, Divine, Jeffrey Jullich, frequent flyers
Syracuse Area Landmark Theater (formerly Loews State), ? and the Mysterians, third party
Joe 1, Commander Cody and the Lost Planet Airmen, Broadway Joe, The Lost Generation, Lost & Found
Joe Amato, Sr. (056-14-9975)

Norm & Gail
JD & Alison
University of North Dakota, Gen X, North Pole, NY, The Ames Brothers, Buffalo Six, Alexander Hamilton
The Jack Kerouac School of Disembodied Poetics, mechas, true believers, Big Believers in...
Rev. Jesse Jackson, Phil Jackson, Hugh Jackman, Joe Jackson, The Book Thing, Punxsutawney Phil
Ted Koppel, Teddy Roosevelt (w/game face), Polly (w/cracker), Coal Creek Trail, Medora, Chuck Jones
Rev. John Shelby Spong (retired), Dr. John, Dear John, John Houseman, John Dewey, Cyrus Field, Ray Hicks,
J. Krishnamurti, Abe Fortas, Six Gallery, Muscle Shoals Rhythm Section, Dr. Lao
Joan Jett and the Blackhearts, Jeanne D'Arc, Jean Marais, Jeanne Moreau, The Island of Dr. Moreau
Wrangler, Senator Bob Dole, the jet set, the echt modernist, the ur-romantic
Lee, Frodo Baggins, Nostradamus, The Vielschreiber Contingent, CHR/Pop, Cosa Nostra
Levi Strauss & Co., WPA, CPSC, Roberto Clemente, Hank Greenberg, Leroy Satchel Paige, Sam Shepard
Lévi-Strauss, Clifford Geertz, James Clifford, James Van Cleve, lifers, Cliff Notes, Ferdinand Porsche
Binghamton University
Amnesty International
The International Mail Art Movement, The Simplification Movement, Poet Laureates
Secret Handshakes International, Planned Parenthood

Idaho State University	*If you insist on hanging*
Joseph Smith	*on my every*
North Penn Senior High	*don't corner me at the*
Liverpool High	*to ask me what on*
Buckley Road Elementary	*I me*

Nate Perry
Luke LaPorta
Eudora (really), Hanging Chad, the 19 (A No. 1), TSOP
Perkiomenville Elementary
Netscape Communicator
A. V. Zogg Middle, WPS1.org
Internet Explorers
Oak Park Elementary
Weatherill Elementary
Central Pennsylvania Youth Ballet
Darwin, Efren Reyes, Kefauver Committee, International Man of Mystery
Allied Van Lines, US Postal Service, UPS, Fed Ex, Amtrak, The Airline Industry, Greyhound
Columbia College of Chicago, Columbia House, Alfred Korzybski
Budget Rent A Car (really), all the King's horses and all the King's men
The Factor, The Schmooze Factor, The Serious Quotient, The Tougher-to-build-than-tear-down Delegacy
Alan Smithee
CSICOP
The Democratic National Committee
The Republican National Committee
The Green Party
The Libertarian Party
The Donner Party, Frantz Fanon, Dale Earnhardt Sr. & Jr., CGI, PDA, SGML, XML, SIM, TABOR, CBGB
Studio 54

Car 54, Where Are You?
The Fillmore East, The Typing Pool, The Blue Grotto, the hit parade, the GI Bill, the French Quarter

19
Frank Zappa, Z-Boys, ZZ Top, knock-offs of all sort, creationists, atheists, bumpkins, suckers, grunts
Harry Carey, Sr., Franka Potente, draft dodgers, COs, punks, brats, juvies, busy-bodies, men-in-the-middle,
monkeys-in-the-middle, know-nothings, fogies, Kami, Denis Rodman, BET, The Lumière Bros.
SCLC, SNCC, know-it-alls, rockists, HNIC, quatroleavians, the Indian Head penny, the Buffalo Nickel
KKK, WIKI
ADL, PLO, CIA, OSS, OSIA, IS, SI, ISO, HMO, HMS, RAF, Lowell Thomas, Thomas Frank, Mack & Mire
Heckle & Jeckle, Jekyll & Hyde, Ship of Fools, beggars, robber barons, flunkies, junkies, ambassadors
East Timor, Somalia, Bosnia, Rwanda, Tanganyika, vixens, dolls, The Wrong Side of the Tracks
Mother Earth, Gaia, Mother Tongue, The Good Earth, The Other Side of the Coin, The Flip Side, The Other
Hand, Father Time, The Sands of Time, Peter O'Toole, Proust, Faustus, floozies, bikers, pikers
Little Sister, Sister Golden Hair, Little Red Riding Hood, Little Richard, Stevie Wonder, Red Adair
Captain America, The Incredible Hulk, Sub-Mariner, The Fantastic Four, Peter Parker, Reed Richards
Journey Into Mystery with The Mighty **THOR**, *Here Comes...* **DAREDEVIL**, *The Man Without Fear*, Tony Stark, Ole
Shellhead, The Invincible **IRON MAN**, Galactus, Kingpin, Doc Ock, **BLADE**
The Red Skull, , Johnny "Ring-A-Ding" Romita, The Caped Crusader, Humbert Humbert
Bob Barker, Don La Fontaine, Laura Riding, Laura Riding Jackson, god's green earth, The Brickyard
Wolfman Jack. Luigi-Bob, Charles Stein, J. M. W. Turner, Junior Burke, Miekal And & ...
House of Dracula, Wilhelm Apollinaris de Kostrowitsky, Merian C. Cooper, Ruth Rose, Chris Marker
Lester Bangs, Town Clowns, Rollo Tomassi, The Martian Manhunter, Wolverine, Prof. Richard Brown
Herblock, Herbalife, Amway/Quixtar, Multi-Level Marketing, Pyramid Schemes, *Yes, we have no bananas*
R. Crumb, Herb Levy, James English, Eric Crump, Joan Osborne
Deadman, Dead Man, Hellboy, Haifa Street, Ebbets Field, Shakira, Xbox366
The Watcher, The Watchmen, Stuart Moulthrop, Miss Hathaway, Matilda (waltzing), Tom Waits
The Thing, Thing
The Thinker
Paul Bunyan, Paul Goodman, Giant, David Horowitz, Peter Piper, C64
Fabulous Furry Freak Brothers, Beavis & Butthead, FMS, The Moonies, ex-cult, Moon Palace, Grauman's
Paul, Paul Revere, The New Guinea Singing Dog Conservation Society, underdogs, Underdog
& the Raiders, Tatyana, Ruth Lilly, Joseph Parisi, Alan Dershowitz, travel agents, bank tellers
Steve Reeves
John Bunyan
Chocolate, Pistachio
Vanilla
Maple Walnut, Medgar Evers, Underwriters' Laboratories, The Man on the Moon, The Man from Mars
Richard Avedon, Angkor Wot, Gala, Godzilla, runway 2-9er, The Bobbsey Twins, El Topo
Wallace Stevens
Jerome Rothenberg & Pierre Joris & Pierre Joris & Jerome Rothenberg & Jerome Rothenberg & Pierre
Joris & Pierre Joris & Jerome Rothenberg
The Great Dimestore Centennial, The Great White Way, The Great White Hope, End of the line—
John Henry, The Hopeless Romantics Alliance, Jerrol LeBaron, Fanny Brice

Henry Hull, Wonder Woman, Lois Lane, Long Cool Woman, Nathan Lane, St. James Theater
in a Black Dress, Emma Peel, COOL 105, KBCO, The Hawk, WAER (ca. 1970), WRPI, LL Kool J, S & L
I Spy, The Huxstables, The Beverly Hillbillies, Baliwood, Dollywood, Bronson, A Man For All Seasons
Frosty the Snowman, Song, Bloomsday, The Watergate Break-in, Iran-Contragate, Branson, The Waltons
Woodstock Nation, Placido Domingo, parsleysage—where my Rosemary goes, Judy in the Sky (w/glasses),
Lucy in the Sky (w/diamonds), Windy, Mary Carillo, The Tyger, Robert Hanssen
Tiger Woods, Captive Wild Woman, Hedwig, The Devil Bat, Doyle Brunson, Typhoid Mary
The Lionhearted, The Heartbreak Kid, Survivor, Survivors, Mimi Rogers, Dudley Moore, Thomas Crown
Jack Lemmon, Tony Randall, James Mason, The Barrymores, Uncle Tom, Patrick Henry, W. E. B. Du Bois
Walter Matthau, Jack Klugman, Jack Warden, Julia Roberts, Mr. Roberts, Mr. F. C. Ware, Heart
George Plimpton, WMAB (Women and Men Against Borderlines), Barry Manilow, The Pentagon Papers
The Just-shows-to-go Partnership, Norm Crosby, Patrick Herron, The Hogerhand People's Front
Woodstein
Woody Woodpecker, under *viagra?*
Woody Allen (appearing as "himself"), Judith Barry, Sadie Benning
Woodland Pattern, City Lights, Molloy, Ern Malley, Mallarmé, John Tranter, Moby, Bridge Street Books
The Village Voice, The Nation, The New Republic, The National Review, The Christian Science Monitor
The Possum Pouch, The Competition, The Establishment, The Antichrist, The Mirror Mirror Corp., Ltd.
Web Del Sol, Steven Clay, boomers, echoboomers
ABR
Rain Taxi, BLT, GLT, BHT, (THE SECRET INGREDIENT)
Reader's Digest
Zaharias, Babe Didrickson
Silver, Long John
Appleton, Crabby, under *virgo?*
Araki Yasusada, The Ya-Ya's, The Hamptons, Fred Hampton, Jr., Maybellene, Frank Bullitt, Dear Abby
Nikki-nikki-tembo-oh-so-rembo-oo-ma-moochee-gomma-gomma-goochi
Monk, Mingus, Miles, Mann, Crispell, Jessica Williams, Trio, Poetry for the People, Dale Dye, Will Rogers

18
Hey Hey We're The Monkees
John, Paul, etc.
George Gordon, Lord Byron, anonymous external reviewers of this ms (whose names i will someday know),
800 lb. gorillas, City Hall, white elephants, Baron Giichi Tanaka, Maid Marion, Gordon Moore
Claude Rains
Rin Tin Tin, Seattle
Slew, The Birds, The Byrds, {   }, Panem et circenses, The Stand-up Poets, the Remant, stand-up guys
Carnak the Magnificent's mind meeting Lenny Bruce's mind meeting Susan Sarandon's mind meeting Steve
Allen's mind meeting Dick Cavett's mind meeting Susanne K. Langer's mind meeting Donovan's Brain
meeting Alfred North Whitehead's mind meeting Jack Paar's mind meeting David Letterman's mind meeting
Art Linkletter's mind meeting David Lynch's mind meeting Sun Ra's mind meeting Mary Daly's mind
meeting Sly & the Family Stone's meeting The Staples' meeting Bill Maher's meeting Phil Donahue's meeting
Howard Stern's meeting Christopher Hitchens's meeting Walter Cronkite's meeting
Elisabeth Cady Stanton's meeting The Grimké Sisters' meeting Dwight Macdonald's meeting Cheech &

Chong's meeting the Capital Gang's meeting Meryl Streep's (as Marvin Gaye's) meeting Cassius Clay 's
meeting Daniel Shorr's meeting John Cameron Swayze's meeting God's meeting Talking Heads'
<html><body><font color=green>Kent Johnson's body (in context)</font color></body>
The Language Poets (in context)
The Nuyorican Poets (in context)</html>
Jeremiah Johnson (in context)
Jack Pierce (on Karloff), Willis H. O'Brien, Ray Harryhausen, Stan Winston, Rick Baker, Boris the Spider
Chopin, Rhode Island meeting Jon Stewart's, Christian Brothers Karamazov, Number 3
Aretha Franklin, The Godfather of Soul, Javier Alvarez, geezers, pink flamingos
Benjamin Franklin
Walter Benjamin, Walter Brennan, MenMenMenMenMenMenMenMen, *Women*, Little
Women, The Righteous Brothers, Phish, Crapp, the poop deck, The Brancusi Trial
The Temptations
Holland-Dozier-Holland
NWA, the last veteran of the Spanish-American War, who died in 1992 at the age of 106
My Dentist, My Periodontist, My Mojo
Radiohead, the Next Generation X Files, Strawberry Alarm Clark, salt of the earth
JFK (Jr. & Sr.)
The Staff of *Z Magazine*, 92nd. Street Y, Free Library, Gruppo '63
Andrew Levy (the poet, friend of the party of the 1st part) & Bob Harrison (ditto)
Patrick Pritchett (ditto again) & Barbara Wilder (etc.) & Oscar Wilde, Plymouth Rock, Jamestown
Noam Chomsky
Howard Zinn
The Day the Earth Stood Still

Jack Collom & Jennifer Heath   "If the production of truth-artifacts benefits society and
Amorosa visione   the world, fine; however, by an entertaining paradox,
Captain Kangaroo   the premature pursuit of this benefit, as such, tends to prevent
Kellogg's Frosted Brown Sugar Cinnamon Pop·Tarts   the foregrounding
Catherine MacKinnon   of truth in the production
OULIPO   of artifacts —
Lyn Hejinian   which generally must be accomplished
Leonardo of Pisa   independent
Our Gang   of pragmatic
Michael Moore   concerns."
Spanky and Our Gang will never be the same, the Yancy Street Gang, the "it" girl
Mink Coat Mob, flash mobs, Ad Reinhardt
Bloods
Crips, Koba, IPO, MSRP, NOAA, Will Geer, Harry Hay, H-a-double r-i-g-a-n spells
The Mysteries of Udolpho
Marjorie Perloff, Gerda Lerner, Samuel Taylor Coleridge, Travis Tritt, Frank Gehry and his staff
Steve, Maria, Alba, & Ava Tomasula
Margo Channing
Jane Fonda
HKF (wife and partner of the party of the 1st part)

17

The Best Years of Our Lives

Mike Amato (brother of the party of the 1st part)

The Party of the 2nd Part

The Red Army Faction

The Faculty at Harvard

Bill Monroe

Shane, come back Shane, come back

Marshall McLuhan's 1st Editions

Paulo Freire's Ghost

Ha

Odin, Zeus, Son of a son

of a sailor, Or stain her Honour, or her new Brocade

Aphrodite, The Vulcan, A Comedy Tonight, Felipe Fernández-Armesto, The War Dept., DOD, NRDC

SONY, Neil Postman, Ivan Illich, Margaret Sanger, Christa Cline

Ho, Ho, Ho Chi Minh, Peyton Place ("She'd like to be a writer. I'd like her to go to college."), Marion Jones

Al-Khowarizmi, Wilt the Stilt, RFK, The Gated Community, The Golem, Ethel Merman, Murder Inc.

Fay Wray, Harry Caul , Bhopal, Frank Kermode, The Cardiff Giant, Dudley Doright, U. S. Forest Service

Merriam-Webster's *Collegiate,* African Queen Latifah, Hays Code, Prometheus, Beatrix Potter, Mod Squad

Bhagavad-gita

The *Koran*

or *Qur'an* in Portable Document Format, *Hadîth*

The Poets' Encyclopedia, anodes, cathodes, anions, cations, opposites, likes, terrorists, freedom fighters

Nicole Peyrafitte, The Baha'is, Hawaii [Hawai'i] Five-O, A & W, DQ, The Forms of Life

Leonard Maltin's Movie & Video Guide, Elmore Leonard, Clarence Williams III, 82nd Airborne, Nas

The Continental Divide, The Lost Continent, A Thousand and One Plateaus, St. Elizabeth's, Lincoln

The Palmer Divide, 55 Cancri, The Ponderosa, An ingenious gathering of poignant leap-

frogging, The Gulf of Mexico

The Milky Way

Michael Joyce, Sven Birkerts, Rob Wilson, Michael Bérubé, Kristin Scott Thomas, Dr. Henry Kissinger, Bill

Russell, Theresa Russell, Gilgamesh, Pee-wee Herman, Superstar, Chomsky, Cary Nelson, Ricky Nelson,

Carrie, PS 122, PT-109, Ken Russell, Leon Russell, Russell Baker, Superfly, Pam Grier, Gloria Gertrude

Steinem, Judi Dench, M, Q, Kurt Russell, Goldie Hawn, Bob Grumman, G-l-o-r-i-a, R-a-g-g-m-o-p-p

Richard Kostelanetz, Richard Dillon, TINAC, WOE, Little Red Schoolhouse, The Writers' Bloc, The

Screensavers, Carlo Parcelli, Joe Brennan, Exxon Valdez, Disney Magic, SubPress, the free press

poetics@, subsubpoetics@, imitapo@, pppoetics@, prosaics@, weallliveinayellowsubpoetics@

Max Steiner, Max & Dave & Louis Fleischer, David & Goliath, The Rock, Rick Flair, peer-2-peer, Chester the

Molester, Sam Spade, Philip Marlowe, J. J. Gittes, Mickey Spillane, Tallulah Bankhead, Andy Robinson, Chris

Rock, Gabe Gudding & Mairead Byrne & Joel Kuszai & Chris Alexander & The Gabors & Arthur Andersen

LLP, Bernadette Mayer, Lisa Jarnot, Mary Poppins, Mary Martin, Mahalia Jackson, Marian Anderson, Shaft,

can you dig it? Eliza Doolittle, Marni Nixon, The Talmadge Sisters, Steve Jobs

Zoe Kona and Alexandros Konas and their folks

Dusty Springfield, Petula Clark, Nous Refuse, The Happy-Go-Lucky Poets, Tamise Van Pelt, Dick Clark

Emeril, The Galloping Gourmet, Giovanni Verga, El Niño, Yaddo, Carmel, The Algonquin, 12 Angry Men

Nilsson, Casey Kasem, Justin Wilson, K. Silem Mohammad, Swiss Family Robinson, Autonomedia
Son of Schmilsson, Oliver, Donovan (Leitch), Liver Lips, Breadloaf, Father Guido Sarducci, Don Pardo, $c^2 = a^2 + b^2$
Diane Cilento, U2, THE SUBJECT OF JOE AMATO'S 2006 GRADUATE POETRY WORKSHOP WILL BE [Your list here]
Tom Jones, Leroi Jones, Voodoo Chile (ca. 1968 and 1984), Carolyn Guyer, Jon Gnagy, E $=mc^2$, Western Europe, The Organ Grinder, CLICK HERE TO UNPRESCRIBE, F $=ma$, The Duke (esp. his comedic side—*North to Alaska*, *Hatari!*, *El Dorado*, *The Green Berets*), Juror #8
Remember the Alamo, Alamo-Girl, Kassia, Purple People Eater, J to the L-O, Frank Gorshin, Loki, Apple Computer, Paul Fix, AOL Time Warner, Dar Robinson, Evel Knieval, Crash Test Dummies, The Judds, JR, Adolph kitsch (MADE IN PRAGUE), The Dalai Lama, The Pope, Microsoft Word 5.1 for Macintosh

16
RiotGrrl, Nimda, Miner 49er, Teamsters, The Tuskegee Study, Kurt Vonnegut (b. 1922), Crash Davis
Goner, *Finger Exorcised*, *Under Virga*
MSF, The Peanut Vendor, Edward James Olmos, Jay David Bolter, Morris Judd, Ruby Dee, John T. Scopes
Big Blue [in 35 argon atoms] Blues Breakers Eliza Joliet Jake Elwood Richard
Brautigan Xerox Blues, Bill Richardson, Ruby Dee, Ossie Davis, Paul Harvey, Don Francisco, Hunter S. Thompson, The Teflon Don, The Dapper Don, Big Mouse, Maciste, Mexico New York Weston
Ontario Cheyenne WY, Vietnam, Blue Meanies, Dale Chihuly, Olive Oyl, Bluto, M-i-c-k-e-y M-o-u-s-e
Fortunate Sons, East Los Angeles Mongols, The Medici, Ho Jo, Super 8, Joe Schmoe, Schoenberg, G-8 Countries Where They Drive On The Left
Edward Said or Ludwig Wittgenstein, E. B. White and Hayden White, FISC, G5
The Structuralists, Poststructuralists, and Culturalists, Harold Bloom or Allan Bloom or Molly Bloom
Frederic Jameson or Isadora Duncan and Dave Dellinger
Jacques Chaka The Wrath of LaKhan, Angelo's Cornucopia, *The New Dictionary of Cultural Literacy*
Slavoj Zizek
The Thing From Another World
The Creature from the Black Lagoon
The New Critics
George Steiner
G.-Albert Aurier
Fat Albert
Steve Evans
Summer,
Fall,
Northrop Frye, Tom Dowd, Grete Sultan, a muscular memorializing
Robert Venturi, Frank Lloyd Wright, Kurt Schwitters, Harryette Mullen, Linda Eder, Ed Bradley
Ventura Highway, Gov. Jesse "The Body" Ventura, Social IQ, Cultural Literacy
Miss Poppycock, Mister Hornswoggle
The "I write this shit. If you like it, read it. Don't expect *me* to" Summit, Sam's Club, Major Bloodnok
Hotel California
Alice's Restaurant

Alice
Charles Lutwidge Dodgson, Alice Liddell, Ray Johnson, Bill Bradley, race traitors, Pat Caddell
Holiday Inn, Linda Brent, Best Western, The Manassa Mauler, Jack Dempsey, Max Schmeling
The Man of the Hour, Prof. Jeffrey Robinson, Prof. Bruce Michelson, Prof. Marty Bickman, Shawn Colvin
A Horse With No Name, The Iron Horse, Marienbad, Prof. R. Baird Shuman, A Man Called Horse
Chet Baker, Big Ben, Big Bertha, Big Foot, Yeti, The Village People, Jeffrey Hudson, Ibn Battutah
L.A. Woman in NYC, NYC in California Girls loved by Mark McMorris @ Naropa 6.11.02, 8:41 pm MDT
The Low Spark of High Heeled Boys, The Soggy Bottom Boys, The Old Boy Network, John Work III
John Barleycorn
John Bull
John Doe
Richard Roe
Johnny Reb
Johnny-come-lately
Johnny-on-the-spot
Johnny B. Goode, Johnny Angel, Johnny Guitar, Linda Lovelace, Art Buchwald, Jacques Cousteau
John Law, Johnny Onions
John Hancock
John Henry
Frederick Law Olmsted, Frederick Douglass, Lorenzo Thomas, Jay L. Lemke, Helen Thomas
All The Young Dudes, Those Who Have Been Omitted at the Behest of Individuals Who Shall Go Unnamed,
Tim Robbins, Jerome Robbins, Hal David & Burt Bacharach, J. S. Bach & Jonathan Livingston Seagull &
Dick Tracy & George C. Scott & Rod Steiger & Spot & The 20th Century & Morgan Freeman & Rocky &
Harry Lime & Expletives Deleted & Neil Young & Tommy & John Sebastian Cabot & The Youngbloods & The
Lady from Shanghai & Ladies-in-Waiting & Michael Basinski & Rocky Horror
The Inocula Club & The "How Many Millionaires Can I Give Birth To?" Millionaire's Club & Basquiat &
The Marshall Tucker Band & Captain Beefheart & Nitty Gritty Dirt Band & Billy Bob Thornton &
The Dolphin Community & The Projects & The Barrio & The Rez & Green Acres & The Joint &
Marlon Brando (as Terry Malloy) & The Rockettes & Dick Morris & frolic intellectuals & Jim Rosenberg

15
Stel-laaaa!
Jim Stark
The Left Hand
and Left-Handed Poets
Action Man, Thinking Man, The Prop Man, The Bogeyman, Sunoco, Shell, Narrator Tony Roberts, KP
Best Boy, Gaffer
Negative Capability, His Dudeness, Buddy Love
Napster (ca. 2000)
Listserv (ca. 1995), majordomo (ca. 1589)
The West Wing (first season only)
General Seating, General Patton, The Secretary-General of the UN, Lt. Calley, old wives, debutantes
Big Brother and the Holding Company
The West Wind, not far behind

Smithsonian Institution, The Psycho-Neurotic Institute for the Very, Very Nervous, no-goodniks
Lotto, The Institute for Creative Technology, Movie Mask, The Aftermath, Sutter Cane, Mrs. Jones
Spooks, G-men, lightweights, NSA, "The Intelligence Community," Tom Clancy, Deep Throat, John Dean
NBA
NFL, AIM, Potus, Scotus, The Long Island Kennel Club
OJ, NCAA, AA, AAA
The Harlem Globetrotters, The Harlem Renaissance, Eva's Man, Sanford & Son, Gerald Rudolph Ford, Jr.
The House that Ruth Built, a millionaire
and his wife,
Mariano Rivera, Geraldo Rivera, low man on the totem pole
The Ump, The Bullpen, The Bosox, *Popular Mechanics*
Hank Aaron
Hank Williams
DAR, Willy Loman, W. Mark Felt, The Congregation for the Doctrine of the Faithful
Ten Years After
Muammar al-Qaddafi, Richard Simmons, Russell Simmons, Bob Holman, WHO, Vector Laboratory
Justice League of America, American League, National League, America's Most Wanted, MVP
Use of Force Model (The Police Safety System), The Pinkertons, The Texas Rangers, Peace Officers
The Police, Keystone Cops, League of Women Voters, Chick Hearn, Jim Hurt (reading this years later)
Dennis Franz, Doctrine for Joint Nuclear Operations
Joe Friday, The Dumb Friends League, Black Dog, Miss Manners, RoboCop, Ripley, League of Nations
What about those Mets?
Pitcher Hill Presbyterian Church
Roseannadu, Rosanna Rosanna Dana, Al Sleet, the hot stove league, the fashion police, the Ashcan School
Theodor Holm Nelson, Mr. Jones
St. Peter's Cathedral (*floreat* 1506)
Alexander Pope & Uncle Toby, the grind house, a sly haunting
Puff (The Magic Dragon), Henry Rago, John Maynard Keynes, John O'Brien
First United Methodist Church, Bob Dennison Ford, Linda Mahfoud
The Huguenots
Bedrock, Norman Rockwell
Billy Graham, "If you're not listed here, you may be listed in a forthcoming project" Consolation Prize
The Dating Game, NASA
IWW
AFL-CIO
Hoffa Sr. & Jr.
United Students Against Sweatshops, Students I've Slept With, Everyone I've Ever Failed, Sylvia Plath
SWP, Everyone I've Ever Ripped Off
Willie Loman, Steamboat Willie, Concetta Franconero, Serge Gainsbourg
Tom Joad
Factory Workers
Service Workers

14

Office Workers
Knowledge Workers
Migrant Workers, Plantation Workers, Brathwaite, Agamben, AM, FM, PM, Sal Paradise, Giorgio, Kamau
Farmers, framers
Peasants, paesanos
Entrepreneurs, undertakers
CEOs, V. LPFM
Wheat Chex, Kellogg's Corn Flakes, Post Shredded Wheat, Quaker Oats, Cream of Wheat, Mother's Toasted
Oat Bran, Barbara's Bakery, Slowhand, All-Bran, A Town Without Pity, *The Atlantic Monthly*
Mother Jones
Low Tide
Engine Engine Number 9
This Old Man
The Williams Sisters & Jennifer Capriati
Raymond Williams
John Philip Dinesh D'Sousa, Hall and Oates
Willie Mays
IBEW
IRE
IEEE
After the Fall
The Dow
Huffy
The Nas
Yamaha
The Mafia, RADA, Emma Thompson, Jane Tompkins, Sir Gielgud (from the head up), ADA
Sir Larry, Sir Ralph (as Lear), Kinko's, Magic Hour, The Organization, The Company, Harley's Davidson Lore,
The Yakuza, The Tooth Fairy, RSC, V8, Teddy Zee, *The New Yorker, Harper's, The Economist*
Zen and the Cost of Motorcycle Maintenance, Fit or Fat, Dumb and Dumber
al Qaeda Operation Manual, Fawlty Towers, Gary Owens, Monty Hall, Jay Stewart, Vanna, The Quiché
Executive Order 12333, 1001B, Atlantis, Palookaville, The Life of the Party, Weird Al, Spike Jones
DSM-IV, SMI²LE, Kirov Ballet, Easy Company, blue-eyed devils, Gina Gershon, Albert Brooks
'Adud ad-Dawlah
Francisco "Pancho" Villa, URL, Ronald McDonald, Tracy Ullman, The Shooting Script
Zeno of Elea, Jo-Jo from Kokomo, Steve Earle, Dee Winchester, F Troop, BlueGhosts, REMFs <lol>, SAC,
Seventh Army, 101st Airborne, Michelangelo, Benvenuto Cellini, Elvis Costello, Leonardo da Vinci
The Salvation Army, El Cid, Paul & Carolee, Susan & Larry, Ralph Lauren, Yo-Yo Ma, Scott Simon, Job
M*A*S*H, The B-52s, Sugar Shack, Tymoteusz Karpowicz, Susan Reuther, Nina Rao, Peter Jungers, Lulu
HIV, ADS, Radio Shack, This Man's Army, Meet George Jetson, Johnny Quest, Beanie & Cecil, The Triads
Hans Zinsser
Hans Brinker
Hans Solo
Hansel & Gretel, herpes?

Advair? William Safire, Sapphire, The U.S. Machine Tool Consumption Report, the registry, Dee Morris
Norton AntiVirus, ebay, The Typewriter Lobby, The Blob, and there ain't *nothin'* i can do about it
Pacifica, Prozac Nation, Acne, Nexium? Gorgo, The Graduate, PAC, James Merrill, Les Demoiselles
H. A. Bourgoin, Make Room for Daddy, Duende, Search for Tomorrow, The Highwaymen, A. Dumas
ACME, A tour de force, The "Why Am I So Optimistic?" Club, The Differently Abled, Sigourney Weaver
A & P, P & C, D & C, Lolita, NORAD, Dr. Kildare, Perry Mason, Freud, Tom Tomorrow, Joan Retallack
Oliver Stone, Ollie North, Greil Marcus, Hegel, snipers, one conservatory of music, Palomar Observatory
Uncle Sam, Uncle Salvatore
Uncle Domenico
Uncle Francesco, Rosario and Antoinette (Antoniette) Amato, Rosario Dawson
4 and 20 Blackbirds, Counting Crows, REM, Dr. John, Lionel Hampton, Tony Manero, Mac Rebennack
Mac Flecknoe
Robert Bly
Captain Bligh (post-mutiny), Captain Crunch (w/2%), Jim Dandy, Billy Crystal, Snoopy, Sloopy (hang on
Nellie Bly
Catherine Graham, Prof. Colbert I. Nepaulsingh, Bert Sugar
Sappho, Pablo Escobar, nosey parkers, the horse you rode in on
YMCA, YWCA, USDA, VVAW, Sharks, Jets, DOS, CPM, Lulu, the free world
VA, NCO, VC, VD, VFW, VE Day, VJ Day, Mad Cow Disease? Hoof & Mouth Disease? Chronic Wasting
Disease? Chronic Halitosis? Tokyo Rose, Peter Rabbit, GPS, LED, OLED, Larry Csonka, Jim Brown
Rosie the Riveter
Edith Piaf
Earthlink, Prudential, The King (out of the bldg.), Col. Tom Parker
UNIX, WYSIWYG
Ma Bell, , Ma Belle Amie, Intention and its disequilibria, Abecedarium Ma Rainey, Gemini, Libra, Flying

13
Saucers — Serious Business, Jodi Foster, Mario, Dario, Apollo, Bessie Smith, Powell and Pressburger, Pa
Kettle, The Guiding Light of Equal Access Accession, Boot Hill, David Keith, Keith David, Netheads
Winston Smith, Winston Churchill, Gen. Omar N. Bradley, Cedar Bar, Western Front, Alfred Leslie
Jane Eyre (as played by Joan Fontaine), Mrs. Ramsay, White Rabbit, Hill 609
UN
Trick or Treat for UNICEF
United States of America
Estados Unidos
États-Unis
United Arab Emirates
The Taliban
RAWA
Amato of Denver, John Denver
Tutti-Frutti Chiclets
Denver Rescue Mission
Simon & Garfunkel
WWF, WCW

NASCAR, NHRA
Both Sides of Joni Mitchell Now
Joe Amato (via amatoracing.com)
Shirley "Cha-Cha" Muldowney, Robert Downey, Jr., Cindy Crawford, Laverne & Shirley, Louis Braille
Barilla Pasta
Jim's Fish Fry
Jim Beam
Gentleman Jim
Heid's
Twin Trees
Mr. Potato Head, Ms. Potato Head, clip joints, fishmongers, Yule Gibbons, Perlo Vita
Flower Children, Wednesday's child + Tuesday's child, John Turturro, The Hollywood Palace, Vera Cruz
John McEnroe & Björn Borg
Jorge Luis Borges, The Guiness Book of World Records, Cascading Style Sheets
Andre at the line, Pete at the net
Jill & Rich & Ron & Bob & Walt & Don & Brad & Carl & Miki & Rick & Tom & Ken & Jeff & Arnie & Al
& Mick & Nancy & Rick & Mark & Judy & Diane & Peggy & Mary Beth & Gail & Sharon & Elisa & Joey &
Lisa & Julie & Steph & Anna & Rae & Lydia & Joanne A. & Hillary M. & ... & Joseph Duemer & David Chin &
Huck & Jim & Bob & Nick & Mike & Dave & Joe & Bing & Bob & Ellen & Jim & Fred & Ginger ... & Jody S &
Greg H & Robin S & Dan M & Derek O & Dennis R & Mary G & Jill H & Michael B & Mark H & Bob &
Bobbye P & George K & Mary Ann C & Ken D & Diane O & Harrison F & Frank L & Dana B & Steven G &
Betsy A & Fred W ... *Notes from Underground,* Mark "[virga is also] a plainsong half-note" Weiss (and his 2nd
ed. *OED*), Beautiful Loser, Muhammad Ali, Mike Tyson, Mark Prejsnar, Hank Lazer,)ohn Lowther, Betty
Boop, Legion of Decency, John & Bernice Mishko
Smokin' Joe Frazier, John Woo, George Carlin, Sandra Bernhard, Dorothy Parker, Robert Parker (tasting)
Columbus Bakery (hot)
Bob Marley & the Wailers, Bill Withers, Grover Washington, Jr., Roberta Flack, Marlee Matlin
Apple Pie
CSNY, CNY, IMF, HUAC, Rules of the road at sea, [Henry] Robert's Rules of Order, Robert Smithson
Tino's Trattoria, Sting (w/makeup), Paco Underhill, Robert Smithson, Pat & Mike, Ellery Queen
Studs Terkel, New Scotland Yard, Robert Smithson, Beaubourg
The Voting Public
The Non-Voting Public, Third Parties, tax & spend liberals, right-wing nuts, liberal interventionists
The Third Reich, The Third Man, The Marshall Plan, *Plan 9 From Outer Space,* White Noise, white sp c

12
Lauren Pretnar & Eric Gleason & Beto Alvarez & Goli Mohammadi & Sam Hranac & Stephanie Preisch &
Ruth Winick & Eric Moffat & Jesus Duran & Sean D. Murray & James Oliphant & Eliza Thomas & Harvey
Millman ... My Funny Bone, Nick at Nite, Warhol, Man O' War, endwar, ficus strangulensis, Richard Gess,
War, The Grassroots, Jared Horney, Eric Moffat, Melissa Barnard, Allison Lott, Brianna Doby et al. Jennifer
Chatel, The Guys with the Blimp, Hellfire and Damnation, Robert Lowell, The 3rd World, The Developing
World, The Civilian Populace, The Other Half, The Indie-Undie Amateur Resistance Crowd, Paul Wellstone,
Guy Lombardo, The Top 1%, Herb Alpert & the Tijuana Brass, Buena Vista Social Club, The Liar's Club, Ruth
Buzzi, Nervous Man in a Four Dollar Room, Jerry Goldsmith, St. Patrick's Cathedral, you're bringin me

down, James West, Kazaa, rolling stones, Weight Watchers International

William Conrad, The Confederacy, The Iroquois Confederacy, Constitutional Convention, Assemblage Assemblage, Artemus Gordon, Hoot Gibson, Amiri Baraka, The First Lady, Fairbanks Jr. & Sr., Lady Luck Gordon Lightfoot, The Pennysaver, The All England Lawn Tennis Club, Theodore Adorno, Loren Eason Stan Brakhage, Stan "The Man" Lee, John Buscema, *Famous Monsters of Filmland*, Ab Fab, Maude Sonny and Cher, Annabelle and Paul, Bonanza, The Rifleman, Napoleon, F. T. Marinetti, Sacco & Vanzetti Sonny Grosso, Steve Buscemi, Jesse James, Frankenstein's daughter, Hisham Melham, Edward Gorey

Campidoglio

Medaglia d'Oro

Nino Manfredi

Rico Bandello, Johnny Rocco, Vick Amato, www.moderntimes.com/egr/intro.htm

Mr. Coffee, Old Vic, the weasel, corporate America, a pretty penny, Rover, Snuppy, The 700 Club

America Cooks

N. & S. Salina St.

118 Maltbie St., 817 Oswego Blvd.

826 W. Belden Ave.

112 S. Dolores Terrace

501 Raphael Ave. ca. 1969

1185 James Court, Napa, Future Home of NAPA Auto Parts Store, Prof. Katheryn Rios, Emily Peros

32, rue Servan, 13 Rue Madeleine, Fleet Street, Marianne, Promise Keepers, Hank Williams, Bocephus

K-Mart, Rush Limbaugh, 248 Parktrail Rd., Home, home on the range

Wal-Mart, Gomer Pyle, Ernie Pyle, St. Lawrence Seaway, Gutzon Borglum, Civiltà Cattolica

bottom feeders, Marshall Field's, Starhawk, monsters from the id, Day-Day, Aleister Crowley

Macy's

MGM

Warner Bros., 20th Century Fox, Paramount, RKO, United Artists

Universal Studios, Monogram Pictures, Toho, Abbey Road Studios, Quincy Jones, Phil Spector American-International, Amarillo Slim, Alhambra Saloon, Matthew Barney, Monkeypox, Angel from Montgomery, Tamany Hammer, Ice Cube, Ice-T, embeds, grown-ass men, TiVo, Paas, WMD, Remulak, Blotto, Ang Lee, hams, perf-poets, SARS, Faith Popcorn, Mike Leigh, Stagolee, Eddie Bauer, Malvo, Sally Menke, Ann-Margret, Abbas, Comédie-Française, Supermax, Hate & Son, a malignant tumor of potentially unlimited growth, metrosexuals, Arlen Ness, Order of the Golden Dawn, NSK, PC, Seymour, The Energizer Bunny, Frank Gotch, The Eddas, The School for Writers, Les Folies Bergère, LLC, Queer Nation, David Boies, Esq., Abraham Zapruder, Mac Wellman, Norath, InkTip.com, the huddled masses, griefers, Will Shortz, carnies, Charles Ruff, Esq., Johnnie L. Cochran, Jr., Esq., Tom Dick & Harry, landlubbers, The Singing Nuns, Michiana, Arklahoma, Judge Roy Bean, Judge Wapner, Bernard Tapei, the fair sex, Edward Burns, Burns & Allen, Levon, loved ones, Mt. Olympus, Delouis fils Dijon, David Hockney (in perspective), the Olympia Academy, Romans, countrymen, James Hilton, The Factotum Fan Conference, The Middle Managers Consortium, Library of Alexandria, groupies, James Murray, David Lee Roth, Kilroy, reform school, The Man in the Street, The Man You Love to Hate, Steve Bartman, Marin Alsop, IMDb, The Carpenters, Lisa Samuels, Bill Veeck, The Middle Mind, IEA/NEA, MoveOn.org, Normal, Illinois, ISU, King of the Road, Bonnie & Clyde, The Writing 69th, Theatricum Botanicum, Bayard Rustin, Mario Merz, Chris & Elizabeth, Kristin & Brian, Randle Patrick McMurphy, Abominists, Calliope, Dr. Atkins, the Zagats, Freedonia, Christendom, HSX Mainstream Poets, mainstream poets, Misty poets, poets, Courier & Ives, Lewis & Clark, Peeping Tom, Burl Ives, Charles Ives, Harold Arlen

Bad Bad Leroy Brown, SY @ Cornell, Where are my teaching evaluations?! It's been 12 years now...
Edward R. Tufte, Lucia Getsi, Curtis White, Genly Ai, Lunt and Fontanne, Allen Funt, Harvey
Kali Tal, Sgt. Saunders, PennMac, Nathalie op de Beeck, Perle Besserman & Manfred Steger
The Postmodern Bag O' Tricks, The Lyrical Ego, The Mask, Lawrence Lessig, Jack Valenti. Yasser Arafat
Grimm Bros. Construction Materials, The Clantons, Kaiser Soze, The Avon Lady, fuddy-duddies
AMAT, Copernicus, The Poles, The Nile, Stonehenge, Mesopotamia, Stratford-upon-Avon, a soda machine in
the rainforest near Mt. Pelée (ca. 1991), knaves, Tim Schellenberg, *The* Gedankenexperiment

11
Mont Blanc and the Seven Valleys
Snow White and the Seven Dwarfs
www.salamandra.com.ar, 99.5 — The Mountain
Roger Corman
IRS
Video Station
American Enterprise Institute
Institute for Advanced Study
Rand Corporation
Animal Liberation Front
The Geek
Homer (when he's not nodding)
Rin Tin Tin
Bijou
Cognac, Deputy Dog
Asbach Uralt
Johnnie Walker (Black), Johnny Ringo, Sandy Denny
Sierra Club, The Wilderness Society, The Nature Conservancy, Richard Lanham, lurkers
Triple A, The "lower limit insincerity, upper limit dematerialization" Club
NATO
NAFTA
Joe DiMaggio, ooh ooh ooh
Epicurus, John Donne, The Weeping Philosopher, The Abjuring Bureaucrat, The Laughing Fool
Dooley Wilson, Schultz & Dooley, next-door neighbors
The Great McGinty, Roberto Duran, Hoyle, neocons, paleocons, lowbrows, highbrows, the booboisie
Garbo (talking), Johnny Carson, Katrina
Knute Rockne, Russell Means, The Jackson Five, Elizabeth Taylor, Keith Tuma, Mark Scroggins
The Fighting Devil Dogs, Reservoir Dogs, The Hollywood Ten, (fight club), The Join-the-club Club
Cujo, Ghost Dog, Three Dog Night, Glen Campbell, The Endless Summer, Mike Douglas, USOP, USO
Sam J. Ervin, Jr., The Sopranos, The Mouseketeers, wildcatters, Baxter Black, Les Brown, roughnecks
and his band of renown, Jesse Helms
Jessica
Jeremy

Gimme Shelter
Shelter From The Storm
Mary Clayton, Clayton Eshleman (w/tiny bandaid on upper lip), Ron Loewinsohn (thank you), The Laramie
Project, DNC, RTF, UWP
Project Greenlight, Ebert & Siskel, Stanley Kaufman, The Project for the New American Century
Francis Ford Coppola
Fred Gardaphé, Diane di Prima, William S. Burroughs, Janeane Garofalo, Alphaville
Dennis Hopper (w/Wyatt and George), *MLA Handbook for Writers of Research Papers* (6th ed.)
John Sayles, Christopher Nolan, Hal Hartley, M. Night Shyamalan, Tara Reeser, Rebecca Kaiser
The Stockade
Netherland Village Apts.
Michael Wilmington
Santana
Gort, Earl the Pearl, The A Team, The A List, Liberace, The Focus Group Group, Espen Aarseth
Chax Press, The Mills Bros., The Life of Emile Zola, National Press Club, SEC, The Electric Company
Anselm & Jane Dalrymple Hollo & Cole Swensen & Carolyn Forché & OED, King James Bible, The Medium,
Ouija and so forth & Anne Waldman & Andrew Schelling & Reed Bye & Steve Katz & Peter Michelson &
Sidney Goldfarb & Trent Lott & Fatty Arbuckle & the gulag & Mosaic Man & Lucia Berlin & Marilyn Krysl &
Lorna Dee Cervantes & Cervantes & Lisa Birman & Tom Raworth & John Reed & The Flintstones & The
Simpsons & The Osbournes & The Old Man & the Sea & Ming the Mongrel & Hell's Angels & NORML &
KirkSpockBones & Dr. J & Myra Breckinridge & Susan Ruether & Larken Ogle & Mike Mazurki & The
Canonized Version (see below) & the Politburo &
Misc. Asses (kissed, & kissed well)
Marcel Duchamp (it goes w/o saying), Marcel Marceau (it goes w/o saying), The Sims
Hostess Twinkies (it goes w/o saying) & Max Regan & Ben Jonson & Ben Johnson & Richard Farnsworth

10
& PIC, don't believe it, it dohhhn't work
& Beemans Aids Digestion
Mother Teresa
& Isabella Rossellini
The Actors Studio, Inside
1968
& Nat King Cole (singing "These Foolish Things"), Lisa Savage, Sarah Haberstich, Johanna Bentz
40 Acres and a Mule & Mabel Dodge & Emma Goldman & Big Bill Haywood, Black Shirts & Post-Fascists
Al Jolson (crooning "If I Only Had A Match")
The Great Man Votes
Angela Davis, Mike Davis, Judy Davis, Judy Garland, Noah (in ark), Philip K. Dick, Baba Wawa
Bart Starr, Ronald Johnson, Robert Johnson, Kant, Sidney Morgenbesser, the fastest pussycats
Kenneth Goldsmith's *oeuvre*, present & future, Longfellow Deeds, SIDS, jolly good fellows
Morgan O'Hara, The Prose of the World, The Bible Belt, Tribe of Ben, The Beltway
Rawlings, "The Mark of a Pro"
Time and Temperature, CFP, the blurb on the back of *Under Virga*
Time In A Bottle, Gary Wright, Stephen Wright (talking to himself from over there someplace)

The Weather Channel, Chief Cook and Bottle Washer, National Whistleblowers Center, David Porush
The Weathermen, Little War Gods, Little Big Man, Little Orphan Annie, Christian Barnard, Rasputin
Country Joe, Joe Louis, Les Paul and Mary Ford, John Garfield, Steven Taylor & Judy Hussie, The Fugs
Sir Peter Blake and Jann Haworth, Keith Abbott, Bobbie Louise Hawkins, Rikki Ducornet, House of Mirth
SDS, Gail E. Hawisher and Cynthia L. Selfe, Christian Bök, Eleni Sikelianos & Laird Hunt, Martha Petry
The Merry Pranksters, The Diggers, The Hippies, The Yippies, The Black Panthers, The White Panthers, The
Blackstone Rangers, The Yuppies, The Bobos, Fiction Collective, Barbara Ehrenreich, Adrian Mitchell
(ca. 1965), Sara Moulton, Connie Oehring, David Strathairn, Brewer & Shipley, The Working Poor, The
List of Adrian Messenger, IRA, The Nortec Collective, Der Sturm, Dogme 95, Seinfeld
Visa, MasterCard, Chase, CitiBank, Patti Hearst, John Waters, Spartacus, Tony Curtis, Big Mike, Burt
Lancaster, Loyalists, Blue bloods, The Dutch Masters, Muddy Waters, Giuseppe Fortunio Francesco Verdi,
Glimmerglass Opera, Good Dogs, Bernard Shakey, Ferdinand Demara, The Boston Strangler, Silent Bob and
Jay, Dr. Demento, EPA, NRC, AEC, FTC, FCC, IAEA, PSA, AAP, OSHA, FEMA, RIP, NB, PS, INRI, CCR, Sly
dogs, The Unabomber, Weird Al, Dr. Kevorkian, Royal Dutch/Shell, ExxonMobil, Free, Bad Company, The
Brown MFA Program, The SUNY/Buffalo Poetics Program, Sylvan Learning Systems, The University in
Ruins, masterminds, masters, slaves, Needle Park, IAEA, Cinecittà, poor slobs
Andy Rooney
Mickey Rooney
The Incredible Shrinking Man
Rita Hayworth
Mike Wallace
Mark Wallace, Lawrence Tierney, Scott Brady, Mr. Blue, Mr. Trolley
You, Dear Reader
Those Within Earshot
Those Within Gunshot
The Fifth Generation L=a=n=g=u=a=g=e Poets, Post-Dogmatists
The Fifth Dimension
Jed Rasula, Vincent Price, Lionel Atwill, W. S. Merwin, Buffy the Vampire Slayer, Jimmy Connors
Sweet Melissa, Sweet Caroline, John Q. Public, Joe Vigilance, Sweet Sixteen, Melissa Etheridge
Grand Guignol, Sweet Sweetback, James M. Cain
Grand Ole Opry, Grand Theft Auto III, The Land of the Free and the Home of the Brave, blowhards
Hannibal, Anthony Hopkins Perkins
American Psychos, Robert "Bobby" Beausoleil aka Cupid, Howard Hughes, Ira Einhorn, Holly Maddux
The Zombies, the devil's advocate, teenage wasteland
Death, and there ain't *nothin'* i can do about it
Dead of Night
Bernard Herrmann

9
Alex North
Henry Mancini, Nelson Riddle, Dimitri Tiomkin, Anne Frank, Dane Clark, Gene Tierney, Darren Brass
John Barry, Michel Legrand, Franz Waxman, Ennio Morricone, Kiki, Weegee, Installation Notes 4.7
Haskell Wexler
Gregg Toland, Conrad Hall, Joe Mannix, the vigilante committee

The Bishop's Wife
George M. Cohan
Public Enemy, Powerpuff Girls, ATF, Mako, The Central Powers, spam, SPAM, fuckoffs, O Fuck Off
Joseph McCarthy, you cocksucker you—and that goes for you too, Pat McCarran
LBJ (walking his dog), Charlie McCarthy, Charlemagne, Jackie O, Mason Williams, Barbra Streisand
Archie, Edith, Gloria and Meathead
Charlton Heston (as Will Penny), Moses, The Ben-Hur Museum, Gore Vidal, MoMA, Amos Moses
The Chicago Eight, red meat
Rich Man, Poor Man
Tommy (JA would like to thank The Who)
American Woman
Who Do You Love?
People, People Who Need People
Fair Weather Friends, UUU (Unfair Use Union)
Every Son Of A Bitch Who Ever Sent Me A Rejection Letter
Every Son Of A Bitch Who Ever Fired Me (5 to date)
The Boss
Patti Smith
The Smiths
Every Pal Who Ever Encouraged Me, Everyone I've Ever Sweated With
Whoever, The Anti-Connoisseurship Anti-DIY Federation of Anarcho-Activists, James Byrd
The Sex Pistols, The Clash, The Cars, The Archies
The King [cowboy], The Little Prince, The Furies, The Sirens, Queen Christina, Standard & Poor's Index
Albert King, Queen for a Day, Regis Philbin, The Faerie Queene, (the late) Prof. Hugh Maclean, Queen, prom
queens, Queenie, The Queen of Sheba, Cleopatra, Early Risers, the fair queen
Late Bloomers, Drama Queens, Dixie Chicks, *American Book Review*
The Tomb of the Unknown Soldier
George Zucco
Dr. Moriarty
Dr. Katz
Dr. Feelgood
Dr. Strangelove
Dirty Harry
The Man With No Name
Pike
The Brady Bunch, The Partridge Family, Buffalo Springfield, La Raza, *The Onion,* Zaha Hadid
Jake LaMotta, Dr. John M. Poindexter, Buster Poindexter, Cannon Mine, Section 8, section XXX!
Martina Navratilova, Diderot (w/d'Alembert), The "I didn't say it was poetry" Mongers, Mike Price
Baron Daemon, Denny Sullivan, Ed Murphy, Eddie Murphy, The Deuce, The Haight, Barry Goldwater
Caravaggio, Martin & Lewis, Gary Shandling, LOTS, M5, Robert Louis Adlai Stevenson, Jack Stanton
Manet, Cézanne, Inspector Clouseau, Vincent, Vince Lombardi, Frida Kahlo, Kandinsky, Louis and Bebe
Barron, Miriam Schapiro, ;-> :-) :-(
007 (ca. 1963)
Secret Agent Man, The Prisoner, The Count of Monte Cristo, John Cage, The Prisoner of Zenda
Anni, Lucie, Audine, Tristan & Max

Joe Amato, Jr. (@ 501 Raphael Ave., above, then)
Adelbert Ames, Jr., Jackson Mac Low, Henry Cowell, *The New York Times Book Review*

8
Yogi Berra, esp. when he talks like himself
Derek Flint
Michael Jordan (@ 40)
Tom Jordache
Nelson Mandela, Nelly
Gully Foyle, AJ Foyt, F. Lee Bailey, Philip Levine, *The Women's Review of Books*
CAGT, Morse Code, Eduardo Kac, Gulley Jimson, Robert Burton
Galatea 2.2, Alan Sondheim, Stephanie Strickland, J. W. Gibbs, The Raven, *The Invisible Ray*
Loss Pequeño Glazier, Shirley Bassey, Roberto Tejada, Count Basie, Debra Di Blasi, Alexander Payne
The Great Escape
Lalo Schifrin
Dietrich Eckart, Twyla Tharp
The Marquis de Sade and/or Ihab Hassan
Jeffrey DeShell & Elisabeth Sheffield, Checkpoint Charlie, The Artful Dodger, Natalie Clifford Barney
Mark Amerika, rated PG-13, PARENTS STRONGLY CAUTIONED, For Violence, Disaster Images, and Brief
Strong Language, Rube Goldberg, The Real Thing, Bee Gees, Sigur Rós, Aerosmith, Liv Tyler, Chris Isaak,
Lance Morrow, Walt Disney, Peter Gunn, Ray Bianchi, Pete Balestrieri as Lars von Trier, Heath Robinson
Lance Olsen, Merv Griffin, Lance Armstrong, Art Fleming, Alex Trebek, Samuel Beckett, J. H. Prynne,
Rosewood, Gregor Samsa, The Garbage Man, Dashiell Hammett, The Agnellis, Roswell, Stella Stevens
Claude-Achille Debussy, Deborah Kerr, Debbie Davies, PG&E, ConEd, ComEd, NiMo, Dillinger's
Dodsworth, Heathcliff
Billy Branch and the SOBs
Brahms Piano Concerto No. 2, Op. 83 (Sviatoslav Richter, piano)˙
Gerhard Richter
Mott the Hoople
Hugh Hefner
Alfred E. Newman (w/1.1.70 expiration date), Alfred Nobel, Your Local Chapter
The Sixth Generation Beat Poets
The Four Hundredth Generation Spoken Word Poets
New (American) Poets
Old (un-American) Poets
Middle-aged (American & un-American) Fiction Writers, New American Optimists, Christopher Lasch
Rachel Loden, Sheila Murphy, Susan Wheeler, Karen Kelley, Laura Wright & Mark DuCharme channeling
Rachel Levitsky, Laura Mullen, Nick LoLordo, Bhanu Kapil Rider, James Sherry, Dodie Bellamy & Kevin
Killian & Susan M. Schultz & Mary Hilton & Sandra Braman & Linda Russo & Jon Volkmer & ... & Brian
Lennon & Jess Seldess & Gwyn McVay & Amy Catanzano& ... & The Blood
of a Poet
O+

˙ The analog recording source for this compact disc was made before noise-
reduction methods such as Dolby were available.

Vanessa Carroll & Amy Wright & Maria Hugger & Susan Duran & Alan Laird & Brian Kenney & Julie
Ascarrunz & Karen Eblen & Charles Blackstone & ... & Joe Farbrook & Mandy Broaddus & ...
INS
Camembert (imported, but of course), Pecorino Romano (Locatelli), Native Seeds ... & Jennifer Moxley
Beatrice (Russo)
Michel Serres
Kenneth Burke
Jules Verne, H. G. Wells, The Four Horseman, The Gipper, Animal, Dr. Livingston, I presume
The Morlocks, frogmen, Figaro, Ken Jennings, Society for Timid Souls
Jennifer-Julu
]mez[, Klez, Susan Howe, James Wong Howe, Elizabeth Willis, Samson Raphaelson, August Highland as
Brian Lennon as Ed Sullivan as Richard Gess as P. T. Barnum as Uncle Milty as Arthur Godfrey as
Dante al dente (w/thanks to Mario Batali) as The Man from U.N.C.L.E., Arthur Danto as Helmut Dantine
The Real McCoy as Lee Strasberg as Stella Adler as Buster Crabbe as Flash Gordon as Red Grange as
The Farmer's Daughter as
Danni Ashe as
John C. Holmes
Sherlock Holmes
Deep Blue
Mr. Incognito
Tim Curry
Bela Lugosi, Coop, Mathew Cooperman, Brian Evenson, Bogey, Gable, Jimmy Stewart, The Carter Family
Martin Landau, Uri Geller, The Good Lord Harry, Mystery Science Theater, E. T. A. Hoffman, Kareem
Cary Grant, Hugh Grant, Lee Grant, Captain Vere, Maxwell Grant, Ricky Jay, The Amazing Randi
Joseph L. Mankiewicz, Richard E. Grant, The Scarlet Pimpernel, Elijah McCoy, Calvino, Edward A. Ross
Hattie McDaniel, Bob Wills and the Texas Playboys, Stevie Ray, Gary Oldman, Jimmy Carter

7
Scarlett O'Hara
George Reeves, Budd Collyer, Christopher Reeve
Kitty Carlisle Hart, George Balanchine, Igor Stravinsky, Louis Sherman, Sean Law, Olivia Chadha
Six Degrees of Separation
James Burke
Dickinson College
Jim Thorpe, Robert Mapplethorpe, Raoul Vaneigem (à la Brian Stefans), Alvin and the Chipmunks
From Here to Eternity
Rambo, John J.
Richard Hatch, John Domini
Swarm Logic
Chili Palmer
Ernie Kovacs
Finnegans Wake, MaMaLuJo, Penelope, Newt Gingrich, *hoi topoi*
The Black Hills

The Black Cat
Evil Dead
Deadbeats
Deadheads
The Exorcist
Charles Olson (*in extenso*, w/Creeley in mind)
Charles Laughton
Charles Coburn
Charles Bernstein
Charlie Chaplin
Charlie the Tuna, Choo-Choo Charlie
Salvatore Quasimodo, Anne Kingsbury & Karl Gartung
Wyndham Lewis
Heavy Metal, slurs for every occasion
Henry Gould, Stephen Jay Gould, Glenn Gould, Joe Gould, John Ashbery, Larry Rivers, Georges Méliès
Le Grand Meaulnes, John Herschel Glenn, Jr., Larry King (live), Sinn Fein, Charlie Rose, Charly
Frank O'Hara
Mina Myrna Loy
Michael Faraday
Jane Addams
Al, Werner, Niels, Erwin, Hermann, Ilya Prigogine, Charles Proteus, Beyle, Benson, The Grinch
Wishful Thinking, Timothy Leary, Moody Blues, Denis Leary, Ron Silliman à la his blog
Hoagy Carmichael (scoring *Stardust*), snake charmers, Shaun, John W. Burns, Able Danger
The Matrix, The Funny Farm, Junior's Farm, Maggie's Farm, The Farm, funny business, VIPs
T. S. Eliot's Estate (stealing?), Charles W. Eliot, Norman Maine, Denzel, Connery, Mel, Camille Paglia, Frances
Gumm, Oppenheimer, Oppenheim, Oppen, N_2O, NLP, DMV, DMX, Wall Drug, Burns Bros., Bob Burns, Ken
Burns, Bazooka Joe, Gidget, Columbo, The Osmonds, Rev. Al Sharpton Jr., RSVP, Sapp Bros., Little America,
D. W.-F. W. -Josef-Carl-Sergei-Fritz-Jean-George-Emilio-Federico-Akira-Anthony-Jean-Luc-Rainer-Lina-
Ingmar-Martin-Mike-John-Stanley-Sidney-Roman-Sam-Lizzie-Jim-Joel & Ethan-Martin-Pedro-Spike-Hitch
à la François à la Peter & Elaine May, Buck Henry, Satyajit, Bucky Fuller, Ochus Bochus, Walter B. Gibson,
Erik Weisz, Fakelangpo, The Searchers, The paparazzi, Arthur C. Clarke, The Association, The Homeowners
Association, Andy Devine, Rosa Parks, Rosalind Franklin, Caetano Veloso
Gumby, Conan, Sinbad, The Warren Commission, Robert Frank, Clarence Earl Gideon that was Poitier too
Abbott & Costello Meet Barton Fink
The Three Stooges Meet Hercules
Boy Meets Girl
Angels with Dirty Faces, Guardian Angels, Axis of Evil, The 9-11 Commission
Joe Amato, New York's #1 Sinatra Impersonator
Karl Marx, *Abbot & Costello Meet Mikhail Bakhtin*
WUSA

6
Soccer Moms
The Mamas & the Papas

Jonathans Rosenbaum and Franzen

google.com|inktip.com|carfax.com|ezwrite.com|porno-search.com|yahoo.com

Sgt. Fury and His Howling Commandos, Aleksandr Gerasimov

Sgt. Pepper, Hatfields & McCoys, Enron, Jerry Vale, Jerry Falwell, Larry Flynt, Robert Goulet, Bob Kane

Jack Kirby, Rev. Jerry Falwell, Cardinal Law, Syracuse Stage, Salt City Playhouse, second string

3rd violin, Frank Robinson, Audie Murphy, G.I. Joe, Second City, the third coast, The MacDowell Colony

Ken & Barbie

"Suicidal Commandos of Faith"

The Thief of Baghdad, Spalding

Vick "I'm in business just for FUN" Lawston

Ole Blue Eyes

The Young Ones

The Cast of *Cold Feet*

Celebrity Den

The Mailwoman, The Milkman, The Butcher, The Baker, The Candlestick Maker, The Acupuncturist

The Massage Therapist, Bruce Lee, ECONCOM, Bizarro Superman, Amanda Stewart, Lauren Myers, Irina Zadov

Chuck Norris

Jackie Chan, Jet Li

Michelle Yeaoh

Witchblade

PEZ

Excalibur

The Green Lantern

The Green, Green Grass of Home, Remulak, Edward R. Murrow

Home Depot, Matthew Shepard, Rev. Phelps, Mr. Phelps, Syracuse Cultural Workers, Dorothy Day

Clem Greenberg, Clem Kadiddlehopper, John Berger, Holly Go Lightly, Giancarlo Giannini, Rip Torn, Jimmy Durante, Louis Armstrong, Robert Armstrong, Il Duce, Duke Mantee, Duke Ellington, Peggy Lee, Christopher Lee, J. J. Hunsecker, Henry Ford, Fred MacMurray, Harold Sakata, Tillie, Present Tense

Ed Harris (as Pollock—you were robbed, Ed; no offense, Mr. Crowe)

Tom Cruise (as Ron Kovic—you were robbed, Tom; no offense, Mr. Day-Lewis)

Dan Rather, Pat Buchanan

Christiane Amanpour

Imogene Coca

Whoopi Goldberg

Jonathan Winters

Robin Williams, Ted Williams (on ice), Robert Kroetsch, Bill the Butcher

Jonathan Williams, Sophia Loren, Elton John, Billy Joel, The Kinks, The Y, Rod Serling, Dennis Farina, Susan Brownmiller, Toni Morrison, William Kennedy, Princess Leia, Princess Di, Indy Spirit, Victory Garden, Dennis Miller (hey, I could be wrong), Sing-Along-With-Mitch, Frank Miller, Art Spiegelman

Bertolt Brecht, Scott McCloud, Western Civ., Gandhi, Sundance, Cannes, Oscar, Emmy, Tony, OBIE, V...-Sing Sing, John Hiatt, Santa, Worldcom, César, William Morris, Fmr. FBI Special Agent in Charge, Shorty Santo, Juno, Razzie

Pauline Kael (reviewing esp. Kevin Costner), Kevin Costner, Elvis Mitchell, Mel Allen, Oliver & Jennifer Rick

Ilsa
Ilse, Mary, Dorothy, Maryetta
Elsa
James Whale, Jack Johnson, Dr. Kinsey, Dr. Spock, Pauline Kael (on TV), Bob Steele, Vegas
The Creeping Unknown, X The Unknown, Irving Berlin, Bandidos Yanquis, Etta Place, Lord Baltimore,
Strother Martin, Diamond Dealers Club, Rad Lab, Edward Bernays, Dixon Steele, Hastings Center
John Huston
Ida Lupino
William Bayer, Alfred P. Sloan, John McDonald, President(-elect) Karzai, Mr. Majestyk, Walker, Alan Sokal,
Cecil Taylor, Mark Turner, Ted Turner, Swingle Singers, Steve Lacy, The Calm, Cool, and Collected, Scat-a-
rap-tap-tap, scooby dooby do, and a-wayyy we go

5
Grammar Checker
The Velvet Fog
Cotton Mather
St. Augustine
Codependency
Ralph Nader
Sor Juana
Paul Robeson
Emmylou Harris, Jerry Brown, Chris Matthews, Judy Woodruff, Mugniyah, Quintet of the Hot Club
Bird, Birdie, La Scala, The Group
A Walk on the Wild Side
The Sunny Side of the Street, Front seat, Back seat, Sabrina (ca. 1954), My Ideal, the backyard, the back lot
The OK Corral, Brown-eyed girls, Blue-eyed boys, The Beach Boys, Beach Blanket Bingo
Eggs, Sunny Side Up; Eggheads; Above Stairs, Downstairs; Uptown, Downtown; small pleasures:
Pussy, Pussy Galore, Anal Sex, Cuntlicking, Orgasm, www.pussysux.com (cookies enabled)
L'Amour, Louis L'Amour, Charles Aznavour, Madeleine et Bob Fosse, The Insider, The Outsiders
Lola, la-la-la-la Lola
la-la land, AC~DC, Honey Rider, Zapata, Charlie and Victoria Harris, Charlie Trotter, Rick Bayless
Sealy Posturepedic
NAMBLA
Richard Pryor, W. C. Fields, The Marx Brothers, Smothers Brothers, Steve Martin, Harry Belafonte
The Joint Chiefs of Staff, Chief Dan George, Syracuse Chiefs, Washington Redskins, APB, Chief Moose
Staff of Life, Pekin Chinks, shirts, skins, guest stars
Falstaff, Weary Willie, Punchinello, Jiminy Cricket, Lambchops, Judy, Joe, Richard Jewell, Eric Rudolph
Isuzu, Mr. Whipple, Jewell, Ross Wheeler, Hell's Kitchen, NDA-21Z, Defense Language Institute, Senate
Spouses's Club, Stainless Steel, Lou Dobbs, the Kitchen, Shore Patrol, cousins, Cousin Jack
The Inclined Plane
Craftsman
Snap-On
Mack the Knife
DL Hand Cleaner, that hp dog under Page Setup..., Texas Instruments (ca. 1975), *these* kinds of poems

Wüsthof
Wayne Gretzky
The Magnificent Seven (ca. 1960)
The Dirty Dozen, The Crazy 88
The Guns of Navarone
Have Gun, Will Travel
Wells Fargo never forgets
Gunga Din, Ida B. Wells, The Time Machine, *Invisible Man*, Maggie May, Conrack, Forrest Gump
Newman's Own, Edwin Newman, Cuba Gooding (Jr. & Sr.), Edmond Rostand, Clark Griswold, Puccini
The Hustler, LMIRL, BYOB, The Brown Bomber
Sundance
Octavio Paz
Robert Rossen, Minnesota Fats, Martin Scorcese, Robert De Niro, Al Pacino, Dalton Trumbo
Stars and Stripes
Body and Soul, The Messiah, Leader of the Pack, Black Rock, Pat Paulsen, Pete Seeger, Ernest Lehman,
David Halberstam, Hannah Arendt, Elia Kazan, Eli Wallach & Anne Jackson, Bill Kazmaier, Nadia, Alexeyev,
Harold Sakata
The Whore of Babylon, Glenda Jackson, Jessica Tandy & Hume Cronyn, Gerber Babies, The Gallant Men

4
Guido the Killer Pimp
Lady Chatterley's Lover
Emmanuelle
O
Mad Max
Max Cady
Case
The Unsinkable Molly Brown, Diana Vreeman
Papa
Oprah, Dr. Phil, Rodgers & Hammerstein & Hart
The Sound of Music, the condition of music
Right & Wrong
the collective unconscious, The Kabbalah, Hershey PA, Kabul, Gram Parsons, Peter Arnett, Abu Ghraib
E.T.
et cetera
Robert Shaw, Eddie Cantor, Pathé, Grasshopper, Bill, Mr. Exhibitor, The House That Jack Built
Errol Flynn (all roles, incl. Custer)
Kevin Kline, Kerry/Edwards, kari edwards, Cicero, Cicero Grimes, Joe Bussard
Rachel Carson, emissions allowances, sooners, Hoosiers, trappers, mule skinners
Sandra Steingraber, The Berrigan Brothers, cris cheek, The Fabulous Baker Boys, Pope John XXIII
Katherine Hepburn, Sammy Davis Jr., Alligator Alley, The Three Little Pigs, Cinderella
Meridel Le Sueur, Isidore-Lucien Ducasse, Isis, Sharon Doubiago, Alice Notley, Barrett Watten, Bruce
Andrews, The Andrews Sisters, (the late) Paul Barrett, Etta, Patti, Australopithecus, The Barbaric Yawp, RWE
The Confidence Man, The Jerk, Archie and Mehitabel, funky town, Stefan Themerson, STP

K'ung-Fu-tzu, Bob Hayes, Lynn Swann, Wattstax, Uncle Ben, Aunt Jemima, Judge Judy, The Creator
Metcalf (Paul and Laurie)
Allen Ginsberg, Justice Ruth Bader Ginsberg, & someone sd something about new valuation theories?
Barbara Schott & Neil Besner, Everyone Who Ever Dropped By For A Beer, Currency Exchange
Doug Barbour, Everyone I've Ever Dropped In On, Doppelgänger, zee author, the barbershop
Aldon Lynn Nielsen & Anna Everett, C. S. Giscombe, my checkered past, Blind Willie McTell, Black Patti
Alan Golding, Sir Edmund Hillary, fellow travelers, the powerful, the powerless, ESP, ESPN, EST
Charles Potts, Joe Tabbi, Randy Petilos, Andrei Codrescu, James Peltz, Maureen Seaton, Holly Carver
Naslima Taslin, Frank Tashlin, Ty Cobb, Gorby, Brown Jug Band, Richthofen's Flying Circus
Christine Levecq, Jennifer Drake, Michel Delville, Philo T. Farnsworth, Stephen Wolfram, Nick Piombino
The Work of Art in the Age of Botanical Preproduction, 20,000+ words/maniacs, Stem Cell Line #48
Norbert Wiener, Beaver, Samantha, Hurricane Agnes, Ursula K. Le Guin, Helen E. Longino
     Heinz von Förster, Mary Richards, Paul Feyerabend, bell hooks
     Donna J. Haraway, I. A. Richards, N. Katherine Hayles, Evelyn Fox Keller
       Allucquere Rosanne Stone, Gerda Lerner, The Virgin Mary Magdalene, Mahler
       Joanna Russ, Robert Loggia, Lucy, Lucille, Otis Blackwell, Peter Elbow
     Samuel R. Delany, Alfred Bester, Rudolph, Nancy, Mrs. O'Leary's Cow, Thomas S. Kuhn
Isaac Asimov, Bonnie Raitt, Fate, Lucifer, Curt Gowdy, Howard, Frank & Dandy Don & *did I already list* Ten
Years After? *how does Robin Trower grab ya?* & Johnny Mercer & The Inspector General & Bernard Shaw & Sir
Lancelot & Medea & The Downwinders & Aristotle & Aristophanes & Old Wives' Tales & The Pied Piper of
Hamelin, and Bashful, Basho, Laura, Carole, Janis Joplin Ian, Ruskin's eye, Myanmar
Monette (my godmother), St. Joseph's Hospital, Dr. Maglione, René Thom, Murphy, SVR, GRU
Suzette
Joseph A. Amato, author of *Dust: A History of the Small and the Invisible*
Joseph C. Amato, Professor of Physics at Colgate U
Bridge of Sighs, (So much depends upon) The Yellow Pages (glazed with coffee/beside the glazed donut)

3
Steve Reich, Aaron Copland, land of milk and honey, works and days, Land of the Morning Sun
My Address Book, Parker, #2 Pencil, H. Behlen & Bro., Kensington Turbo Mouse, Reverse 911, Mac iici
SNL, MTV, VH1, CSPAN, PBS, PPV, DDT, PCB, PCP, LSD, LDS, HDL, LDL, HBO, MIA, KIA, HRT KOA,
Monty Python's Flying Circus, Sybil, Cybill, Eve Black, Adam West, The Bandit, John McClane, skinflints
Big Mac, Fries, Coke
Whopper, Fries, Coke
J. Wellington Wimpy, KFC Bucket, The "What we think we're doing *is* what we're doing" Movement
Chorizo & Potato Burrito, smothered; The Chora Chorus, Robert Reich, Blind Spot Industries ®, © 2003
Raul Julia (w/stogie), Horace, The Oracle at Delphi, *The Odyssey* (trans. Robert Fagles), Mark Bernstein, Joe
Montana, The Better Part of Valor, Dried Figs (Greek *or* Turkish), Open Source Movement, PRB
Cottonelle (twelve-pack of double rolls), Yoko (brought her walrus), Rough Riders, Dear Prudence
The Rat Pack, The Brat Pack, The "We can't or won't separate the wheat from the chaff" Coalition, 401K
Camel (unfiltered), The "I wouldn't want to belong to any club that would accept me as a member" Club

Mary Jane, *Mary Mary, Quite Contrary* mixed with *ABC, Easy As 123* (pizz.), Frontier Days, Tracy Chapman, Inmates of Every Stripe, Scarface (ca. 1932), David Byrne, Funk Bros., The Fellowship, CK Cream, Annie Lennox. Satchmo, Liz Phair, Julia Child, Paul Bocuse, Tom Mandel, Ed & Jenny Dorn, José Feliciano, Toni Morrison, Johnny Depp, Jacquelyn Fox-Good, Sherri & Artie, Woody & Arlo, Tom Dooley, Opus Dei TNC, MBU, RWS, Shawn Fanning, Red Rock Eater News, Jim McKay, The Hermanator, The Terminator, William Gass, Batso, Sheryl Crow, The Colorized Version, The 2nd Revised Standard Version, The Edited-For-Time-And-Content-And-Formatted-To-Fit-This-Screen-Version, The Abridged Edition, The Norton Critical Edition, The RCA Victor Gold Seal Edition, The DVD Collector's Edition, The Braille and SAP and Closed-Captioned-For-The-Hearing-Impaired Editions, 26x62 lines/hr? 21 voices? 20 questions? 1st Amendment, Bob Seger, Whom Spacetime & Memory Haven't Served (& w/apologies), Who Also Serve~
      Arnold, Matthew, 100,000+ real characters   ~And Now Presumed Dead
Neville Brand—in fact *all* of Stalag 17, Vannevar Bush, FDR, Ike, I'M FOR NIXON, KGB, Mikhail Gorbachev, Mel Brooks, Peter Boyle, Jesse Owens, Jackie Robinson, Bojangles, Dorothea Brooke, Cate Blanchett, Jack LaLane, (Sir) David Frost, Edison, Maya Lin, words like *gazetteer*, Mr. Magoo, Ronald Reagan, Warren Zevon, Bush (Jr. & Sr.), Skull & Bones, Saddam Hussein, Dr. Evil, Osama bin Laden *(see the new bin Laden video at cnn.com)*, Aladdin Sane, Fu Manchu, Jack the Ripper, Cruella DeVille, Lassie, Lee Harvey Oswald, Sgt. Raymond Shaw, Son of Sam, Tommy Udo, Timothy McVeigh, Cody Jarrett, Uncle Joe Stalin, Noah Beery (Sr.), Trotsky, Col. John M. Chivington, Montagu Love, Pol Pot, My Lai Low Tech-High Concept Lynching Dr. Mabuse Fat Man and Little Boy Attica SPECTRE MAD COINTEL PRO, Liège CHAOS SDI˙ Weapons of Mass Destruction Black Thursday no Tuesday no the Stallion Herbert Hoover Pac-Man Black September CREEP WTO Inner City K-12 Bugs Bunny & Friends Mr. Peabody Mr. Metzger Edward Everett Horton Eliot Weinberger Elisha Cook, Jr. Exchange Students Wild Thing All Who Are Made Victims, All Who Would Wreak Havoc, All Who Would Seek Vengeance, All Who Would Object Conscientiously, All Who Would Conduct Diplomacy, All Days That Shall Live In Infamy, The Good Old

2
Days, auld lang syne, The Golden Years, Happy Days, Salad Days, A Thousand Points of Light, The Pointers, Seurat, Bill Clinton, Monica, Tiny Tim, Mario Cuomo, Carly Simon, St. Mark's Poetry Project, Dirty Bomb, The Venona Project, The Manhattan Project, Bill Readings, Alfred Stieglitz, Martha Gellhorn, James Agee, Federal Inmate No. 55170-054, Ferdinand Foch, The Dogs of War, Robert Browning, Jonathan Schell, N.N., Jeremy Rifkin, Crazy Horse, Rebecca West, Grand Funk Railroad, Mujahedin, Basidiomycete, Blake, Bull Durham, Sitting Bull, Iron Eyes Cody, Ginger, Norma Desmond @ fade-out, the Solar Hygiene Council, the Solar Logos Foundation, The League of Lepidoptera Lovers, Alvaro de Campos, Elmira Gulch, Zorro, NVA, Cicciolina, the Mayans, American Volunteer Group, America a seconding near
simultaneously, silently even
of, by, or for countless other persons, places, things, ideas and
personification, the scheme of things evidently too
ghosts evidently too, names and titles and events and feelings and aches & pains and practices, practiced delu]g[ions too stupefying, too wondrous, too copious evidently to renounce
or reproduce, cruel & kind, strong & frail, black & blue & grey & brown & yellow & tanned, animate & rich & inanimate & phony & semiconscious & ugly & heavily-armed & sentimental & tall & tedious & serious & meretricious & red, mythical & bigoted & substantial & inhuman & demonstrative & attractive & partial & courageous & funny & smart & dumb & deaf & foolish & learned & senile & fat & fit & green, cliquish & fuzzy & petty & hunkered down & noisy & ill & overjoyed & bare & modest & twee & homeless & ambitious

---

˙See *Justice League of America* 15 (Nov. 1962) for one of many conceptual precursors—which just happens to be one of the earliest comic books the author can recall reading.

& atomic & lovely & shy & opinionated & dry & tired & pompous & uneven & generous & rude & unfaithful & glossy & filthy & hot & true & cold & failing & charismatic & banal & loyal & prolix & hangdog & dull & disabled & tweaked & clumsy & enlisted & congested & graceful & violent & apprehensive & egotistical & fictive & yearning & appalled & friendly & determined & ragged & erudite & ecstatic & inexorably local & mindlessly global & unrepresented & frenzied & intractable & bilingual & resistant & skeptical & resourceful & musical & asthmatic & nimble & young & changing, ever [you would say] changin

10

November

<u>And A Parrr-tridge And A Pear Tree</u>

Sometimes the context (e.g., laugh track) *is* everything.

Sometimes not.

Sometimes content (e.g., having teeth) *is* more important than form (e.g., grinning).

Sometimes not.

Sometimes saying (i.e., remaining silent) *is* more important than not saying (i.e., remaining silent).

Sometimes not.

And sometimes we scribes can be too, uhm, cute.

She loves me not.

Sometimes things fall
out, adjacency means
not a goddamn thing, or
how should I know?

She loves me.

Pass me the binary
turkey. The work's now
in the bag.

Now. Now
this -

Oscar

<u>Read All About It</u>

So there I was, as I say
under virga. There
we were. And we were, the both of us
                          (asthmatics)
sick from
                    [of]
and in denial   ↑
the drought, the worst
"on record," esp. vis-à-vis my tenure
record, in the land apparently
of too many uses
for too many
at the wrong moment
of climatic or
cinematic
"history."

          (Have glossed this elsewhere
          and more succinctly, having
          done research
          for the movie, again.)

          ("You need to know about the drought
          if you're an easterner or midwesterner.
          The west is drying out at an alarming rate
          and this will have long-term consequences
          for easterners and midwesterners
          and westerners, the many transplanted
          and what relatively few remain
          of the vitally indigenous."

                          Abraham Lincoln, 1859)

Up here it's somehow so much clearer
that there's a bastard for every nationality
or group, so defined. Creative writers
for instance. Transplants, like
us. Or Italian Americans
who, around here and aside
from a few enclaves, frequently become subjects
of conversation.

Well I get that back east too, in spots.

This elevation provides ample
perspective, at any rate. For example
a book, one realizes, is like a year
                    (a book a thing
                    having duration
                    and more)
subject to revolutionary
orbits. On Earth a book is thus & so
long, like a year, yet on Mercury
an Earth book
                    (the only book we Earthlings seem to recognize, yes)
appears so much longer
                    (i.e., and to torture (torture)
                    an analogy, Mercury's orbit
                    being so much shorter
                    hence it would take more Mercury years
                    to read an Earth book
                    than Earth years)
while on Mars
maybe half as long. The further you get
from the light source
the shorter the book seems
and at the outer reaches
of the solar system
it's a mere fraction of its heft
                    (takes no time at all to read, heck
                    you can't even make out our
                    bluegreen orb
                    with the naked eye)
and our years, by comparison
seem puny, like us.

Further, some who dwell at these mighty elevations
                    (including those of higher learning, truly)
interpret their enhanced perspective
as endowing them with special
powers—the enlightenment, we shall call it
                    (i.e., in our more judgmental
                    and cash-deprived
                    moods)
of the perennially unenlightened, the sense
of being so much closer, closer

to the light.
                    (if only a mile or so up
                    unless you're climbing)

This is, strictly speaking, an empirical assertion
on my part. And recall that there's a bastard
for every nationality
or group, so defined.

                              Flatland bastards have no such heady
                                  aspirations. For them, it's all pick
                              & shovel work. And in the Syracuse
                                                              I knew
                                                they might pelt
                                              the visiting team
                                                 with oranges.

There persists, too, a glacier hereabouts
                    (shrinking
                    from what I hear
                    tell)
so proximity can be deceptive
if your objective is a fire
in the belly, though some, I daresay
will be only too happy
to look down upon your
book, your fire, your
                    (let us daresay)
demonstrations.

And what brings such as these
to comport themselves
so handily
                    (i.e., with opposed thumb
                    and forefinger counterpointing
                    my synthetic middle finger)
in such a region?

A frenzied lack of imagination, courtesy
of a steady wage. And of course the desire
to be closer, closer
to the light.

This is, strictly speaking, a creative
                    (if sentential)

account on my part, one that would
                    (prompted by a thorough, highly dramatic
                    ass-reaming)
map the migration
of the uncreative mind
as it gropes
toward its creepy legacy
of career and final
resting place.

For "account" substitute "hypothesis," and reread
without half & half.

From what I hear
tell, one tries
one's best
to appear ridiculous
during episodes
of frank generosity. Then
and only then
one harpoons one's critics.

[He's phoning it in.—Ed.]

Today, I call such as these
                    (i.e., of creepy legacy)
by their last names
and after speaking their last names, first
to last
                    (each spoken as an oath
                    against creation)
I could just
discharge some

                                        spit

and move on.

(No, Italians don't get mad. They get
Oscars for getting mad.)

Papa

Subject To Revolutionary Orbits

Give a listen to the 1954 Nobel acceptance speech.
                        (i.e., in literature)
Aside from the existential
overtones, damned if reaching
for that which is "beyond attainment"
isn't his primary point.

And how did Marvin, a pro
                    (like me)
put it
about bastards?
                    (like me)
"Yes sir. In my case
an accident of birth. But you sir—
you're a self-made man."
                    (ca. 1966)

"So he steals lines."

I said *weeding*, not
reading.

Nothing, nothing
personal.
                    (see below)

Quebec

(You may fart
during this episode.)

"If you know something
in your bones
is deconstruction
yet a possibility?"

First, you must be willing to cut
to the bone.

"And what is the other
of bone?"
you ask.

I posed this question to the good people of Quebec
                    (my cousin Dan's wife Thérèse
                    hails from Quebec, for starters)
one unseasonably warm Tuesday
late in an unreasonably happy December
and they responded, to a person
by pointing to my unzipped fly.

They were telling me
without saying so
                    (if I may be permitted the liberty of translation
                    from *le français*
                    sans phallic
                    or Gallic
                    if not phatic
                    overkill)
that I had rocks
in my head.

Rocks.

The answer is
certainly. Like
evolution.

65

Romeo

AKA L=I=T=E.

And so it has come to this, then
the love of it, wherefore
when you get right down to it
we get it down to
a science,
                    (of all things
                    and note that dangling comma)
this thing(ness)
called poetry, an exact, goddamn'd
science, like physics, like
torture, like
etiquette.

Were the light in her eyes
to go out
I would not stay the course.

Were the light in her eyes
to go out
I could not stay the course.

Were the light in her eyes
to go out
would have only incidentally to do
with the history of celestial bodies
                    (esp. the sun, the moon
                    and the stars, in that
                    order)
would extinguish light's essence
that minor detail detailing evidence
                    (cf., "All light is relevant to each light
                    & each light to every light")
of things seen, unseen
                    (and here, one might interject unsighted, equally secular
                    variants, as the unsighted are only
                    too aware)
but for a single, unfolding
optical event to mean
the world
or its absence, but for

this optical event, its presence
or absence, this second
by second amplitude of living
would end, would mean
that light had been assigned
its end, would have quit
its ends, the end
of all light, the dull ache
at the reaches of all love, a fact
that I would know, would
have known, which end or
fact I would
not want
to have known:

In which event
I should not
stay the course.

That's the theory, anyway. A light supper
will be served at nineteen hundred hours.

Sierra

> Roy Earle is sprung from prison by Big Mac, an old gangland associate who
> wants him to go to California to engineer the holdup of a fashionable resort
> hotel .... His flight is halted by the police and, trapped on a mountain peak,
> he is killed.
>> *Bogey: The Films of Humphrey Bogart,* by Clifford McCarty

Owned the book
published in 1965
since I was a kid.

> (book jacket
> now lost
> to time, or
> the times, the
> relocations
> of sediment)

Saw the movie
even prior, I'd say
I found Bogey
oddly out of character
as "Mad Dog" Earle

> (this is a good thing
> if you know his
> career).

Was it those grey
sideburns, the insinuation
of age, the onset
of sentiment? And Ida
Lupino, Ida
Lupino, I'da
loved her
as a kid.

It's annoying when literary artists

> (remember
> the other dog, that little fucker?
> what was his name?)

"discover" a B+
or D- movie, even
a better-than-average B+
or D- movie, one

you've been watching, it seems
all your life, and try to make
                        (more)
art out of it
for—is it
the one, or the many, or
the many who would yet be
one?

Dontcha think
friend?

"—*unless your words are a way to a better life.®*"

Etc. And STOP using words
you don't understand (e.g., "communication").

You can tell:
                        I am rapidly approaching the point
                                (too much in love
                                with his own facility
                                for abstraction and
                                generalization)
at which I should stop being
or pretending to be
                        (in the neighborhood of)
a teacher. But a decade
and a half
may be upwards of
too long
to do some things, persist
in some occupations.

Dontcha think?

Nevertheless,

"Learn from me."

Nevertheless,

"Hire me."

Nevertheless,

"Let's get high-
er together."

"You won't
regret it."

I just got my flu shot
all's right with the world
of monied elites.

Nevertheless, be not clover
a weed?

Nevertheless, I'm in
clover.

Besides, I have less and less
to say, to earn?
the older and wiser you
and me alike, pal
get.

"Here she comes, shifting, the
blues."

"I admire your courage, Miss—uh—?"

 "You say you write poetry
for adults, but you mean poetry
for smug adults, and I hear poetry
for young adults. You suck
ass, kid, you and that smug
horse you dropped out of
and my dreams of passing glory
shall continue unabated
amid this ambush of smart
alecks, inner children who laugh
at their own jokes. Unlike most
my myth feeds on plenty
of whole grain but doesn't
shit itself."

Bang.
Bang bang.

And remember, always
remember, you fool
it takes two to

Tango

"Say, what do you call this
anyway?"

"There's such a thing as being too
versatile. Or patulous. Or, it's so bad
I couldn't put it down."

Thanks Ron.

He
                              (i.e., I)
thinks
                              (think)
one needs must be more
obscure, yes, more
WW II? Mending
the lifeways, then, heartless
returning to the heartland
the dangling modifier appears
to signal grammatological
                              (i.e., "amato with a
                              self-aggrandizing
                              difference," where
                              metaphors of writing, specifically
                              reading, collide, up-
                              ending themselves
                              in the tomato sauce
                              momentarily exterior to which
                              one interiorizes an "mmmm")
perspective, the embodiment
of his failures not
unlike a pie, a custard pie
that has risen
only to fall, hence not rising
at all to the greatness
once thrust upon it—i.e., the gapingly
paparazzied
                              (from the Fellini
                              film)

face; not unlike that stubbed
great toe that draws all
of your attention
to little avail; not unlike that
just like that the
troubled encounter
with a smidgen of
What Thou Mightst
Have Been, sapping
thy middle-aged ambitions
of the magnifical.

Damn. And this despite a literary library literally littered with literature.

A failure of means ends
with the gratuitous justification
of means?

"Am I being fair?"

"No
fuckhead, you're not."

Some of my colleagues, some of whom
are poets, some of whom
I count as friends 1234
maybe 5 are clueless
about collegiality, that share-
and-share-alike of allies
allied with some institution
who work in concert
to allay the harsh realities
of cash flow
and the like.

Break out the pies!

It's a surplus
of signification
oneway ayway orway ethay otherway [cough]
l'une ou l'autre manière [oy]
one (or the other) that
you can learn from ~~or~~
~~from which,~~ if you still have
your alletway.

73

          (check
          why don't you)

"Just don't make
a habit out of it," she warns, as I plus
size for maximum
cornering, expiration
date suddenly 07/09. Me
I mean. Like magic. Computational
magic.

Praise the lord and pass
the bottle
Mack, cry me
a river, Jane, in other words
baby
miss me
and my Pearl
Harbor antics? That life, that's life
they must have led, those two
before my memory
of them began to
"take shape."

"An entire generation
of writers
is losing its legacy
to its defunct hard drives."

Or will there yet be paper
enough to pore over, to gauge
future life? See that sky, recycled
but holding steady
at 90 brightness?—try, just try
to touch it. By Christ, I've found myself talking
like a trooper these days. *Trouper?*
Trouper. Using the expressions
my old man used.

:   I can't stand people
who live in the past. I can't
stand people who
have no past. I can't
stand
          Are you going back

for the funeral?

Ameri-
ca

                    (mouth
                    agape, sarcastic
                    even, repeat
                    after me)

Ameri-
ca

Huh?

Are you going
back?

Ameri-
ca, your remote
side can be
murder
on our hands
and feet, we
who are your
torch song?

Hardly. I didn't say
I loved the guy
but he's a fuck-up.
I said he's a fuck-up
but I loved the guy.

Sometimes. Pre-1954, port
and starboard, one heard AbleBakerCharlieDogEasyFoxGeorgeHowItemJigKingLoveMike
NanOboePeterQueenRogerSugarTareUncleVictorWilliamX-rayYokeZebra

We can locate other lost codes, other
conflicts. And your
little dog, too.

Uniform

Have a taste
ideological
Use your head
ideological
Sign your name
ideological
Shed a tear
ideological

Take a hike
ideological
Ride your bike
ideological
Use your brush
ideological
Make a fuss
ideological

Say goodnight
ideological
Say your prayers
ideological
Brush your teeth
ideological
Wipe your ass
ideological

Go to work
ideological
Read a book
ideological
Call a friend
ideological
Make amends
ideological

Academic
ideological
Academic
ideological
Academic
ideological
Academic
ideological

ideological
Plant a kiss
ideological
Fly a kite
ideological
Cash a check
ideological
Save your soul

ideological
Shoot your gun
ideological
Just for fun
ideological
In the air
ideological
Everywhere

ideological
Act your age
ideological
Feel your way
ideological
Move your feet
ideological
Life is short

ideological
Eat and run
ideological
Write a pun
ideological
Sing a song
ideological
Cain't be wrong

Academic
ideological
Academic
ideological
Academic
ideological
Academic
ideological

Own the best
ideological
Buy a house
ideological
Mow the lawn
ideological
Feed your pet
ideological

Make a mess
ideological
Lay to rest
ideological
Watch a flick
ideological
Take a pic
ideological

If it's not
ideological
It's no less
ideological
If you like
ideological
Then you'll love
ideological

So don't fret
ideological
It's no sweat
ideological
Just don't trust
ideological
Not to rust
ideological

Academic
ideological
Academic
ideological
Academic
ideological
Have a popsicle
ideological

Victor

Dear Victor,

You can call me Montagu
if you must, Mr. Hitchens
                    (see below
                    and above)
but at times your sense of (ahistorical) responsibility
conflicts with your keen understanding
of historical causality, not least because we all know
that global ideologies intersect, and what's bad
for the soul in one
is likely complemented
by what's bad for the soul in another.

That said, yes, those suicide bombers
are deranged souls, you bet
and no amount of ideological causality
"justifies" their ideologically, if certainly
not air-, conditioned
actions. That makes me
an interventionist, like you, awakened
from Craftmatic®, if not dogmatic
slumber by your presence at our pedagogically
if not ideologically
right-of-center campus on 10.11.05.

I'm just funnin' with you. Or
agin' you.

Still, the inexorable loss of presence
in our failure to swap epidermal layers
to see and feel who we really are, ought to
have been, be:

No I'm not really here
in this romp (having to write
uninspired handling of "uninspired handling
of original footage") not really here
in these words, nevertheless
incumbent starters all
and spoiling for a fight
over anything but aesthetics

or departments
my race is killing me and
yours is probably killing you too
even if it's less murderous
sìչ

Do we want to read and write the poetries
that do the greatest good
for the greatest number?   *Is it worth the paper*
                                                         she asked me, polemic written all

over
her   fonts
It's not an issue, but   *is it worth the paper it's printed on?*

at issue. And that's not
a question? What I want
(if I may)
is a frame of reference
similar to my frame of reference
so that I'll be understood
to be saying
what I'm saying.
You too?

"How extremely stupid
not to have thought of that."

(Thomas Henry Huxley in response to his friend Darwin's theory of natural selection.)

"We must therefore advise
against pursuing a patent
for this nonetheless useful and novel
literary event
due to its failure to meet
the statutory requirement
of nonobviousness
along with a certain absence
of zombies."

"If it's yellow
let it mellow
if it's brown
flush it down."

No, this last is not
a mondegreen, m'lady—it's
Ye Old Woods Saying
another way of saying poetry
for mummies
(if you'll pardon a harsh bit
of empathic Orientalist hyperbole)
sometimes brings out the roadside bomber in me
(if it's not above my pay grade
to say so).

Meantime, dig it, we have the
poetry and jazz contingent, is
that it? But how do I translate, is
that right? the sound of my nose-
blowing in the shower
each morning?—is
that so?—which to my mind
comes as close to Dexter
Gordon as yours truly
is likely to get.

YAWNK?

Ach. Another savage entry
for a savage century—*when*, OK, *uncle*

STOP THE PRESSES

Most old men cry
more often than most young men
cry, to state a nontrivial
fact. What do you transpose
would happen if the numbers
were supposed? Anyway, tears
like tears, may be
a simple process
of accretion.

Whiskey

<u>Circa 1955, abr. vers.</u>

Bottoms up. *Soldier of Fortune*
my primary point of departure
presumably takes place in Hong Kong
and vicinity
The Day the Earth Stood Still in Washington DC
Gunga Din in India
Shane in Wyoming
Gone with the Wind in Georgia
The Wizard of Oz
                              (the sound version)
in Kansas
                              (and Oz)
The Adventures of Robin Hood
                              (with Flynn)
on the sceptered
                              (and oft-metred)
isle
Casablanca in Morocco

and a similarity inheres across these eight films
Gable in both films seeking money and adventure and romance but meting out
justice in a measure of freedom
for Gene Barry
                              (of *Bat Masterson* fame)
and Leigh
struggling to survive but finding
justice in a plot of land and Grant McLaglen & Fairbanks
Jr. seeking adventure and ultimately British colonial
justice Rennie
                              (also in *Soldier*)
an alien
seeking interplanetary
justice Ladd, the gunslinger, seeking frontier
justice Garland, a castaway seeking refuge but first for her three friends interpersonal
justice Flynn, a former Sir seeking courtly romance but first
for his (Crusader) king and country
justice Bogey, seeking
romance at first solitude second but eventually
with Rains and Henreid and Bergman for their country and
"the world"

justice

and prompted to query the nature of such
not country, no
                ("I don't like the country—the crickets make me nervous"—Terry
                Malloy)
such justice
as such
I'm thinking of Abbie Hoffman here too
at the end of that BBC documentary
                (*It Was Twenty Years Ago Today*)
qualifying that Beatles lyric, "All you need is" etc.
and maybe "We don't need another
we don't need to know the way" etc.
esp. after GB's 41
and 43 et al. incl. heebies etc.
and speaking, after tea, too quickly
                (Number One Son Luke
                in *Love Is A Many Splendored Thing*)
of absurdities (as above, *here*), perhaps, nevertheless
I find, on the part of its seekers
as I've constructed them
and note that variant of
justice that structures Ford's *The Searchers*
                (not nearly a sufficient answer, no
                to indigenous peoples, and yet, and
                yet)
honorable men or women or
no
self-deceived or
no
part and parcel of abusive abrasive
abusive power structures like
global PR or product placement or
your link to better communication or
66 low Earth-orbit satellites or
1 office for every 300 Fortune 500 workers or
3000 IP addresses for each
atom on the surface of the planet
                (the news today, *Chicago Trib* 17 August 1997
                oh boy)
or, for an inkling of its capacity to subsume
please do check the etymology of
"bureau" or
no

whether 1955
or 1939
1861
or 1350 and
please do keep in mind this is Hollywood now
utter fiction

in any case I find the presence of something like
villainy
                    (not to put too
                    fine a point on it
                    but some in the US
                    executive branch qualify)

Username _____ Password _____

and anybody ever seen *Out of Singapore*?
a 1932 sixty-one minute flick with both Noah Beery
Sr. *and* Montagu Love, the two great villains
of the silent screen
together and as William K.
Everson puts it (*The Bad Guys*) "one of the deathless moments
of cinema!" and
whether in Hong Kong
or Sherwood Forest
North Africa
or Washington DC
Chittenango (the birthplace of Baum, a half-hour's
                drive southeast
 of Syracuse, my birth place
in - check it out - 1955)
or India
Atlanta
or Kansas
Jackson Hole
or Singapore
or Montgomery

whether on the planet Earth
at Tara
in Rick's
in Hyde Park
                    (i.e., Chicago
                    where we lived, Kass and I
                    or me, as I am wont

to say, when I
or me first composed the
longer version
to present at the Cross-Cultural
Poetics conference
at U of Minnesota, 1997, organized
by Maria Damon, Fred
Wah, nice chap, nice
enough to thank me after
for my anger; this is the first
and only time I met Armand
Schwerner briefly, too
briefly. Is *this* what you call
community building?)

or somewhere
over the rainbow

I locate an operating principle of
not degrees
of separation but of
                              (as if to counteract)
justice

And what is justice
without the action of justice?

Yes, this is an appeal.

To witness violence.

To witness violence.

justice, to do
much ado, indeed
                              (not revanchist, no)
inseparable from somebody or other's capacity
to act responsibly
if not a willingness to, if not
at the very least the presumption
on the part of somebody
or other

further, that said principle
or, better
or worse, its representation

prevails
in the popular literature
                        (incl. film)
even as this presumes
upon the contours
of the other
who is to be subject
to such
justice, to such
necessity—

Hey, it's something, uncle.

and to act so however self-deceived or
conjectured or
engaged or
disengaged or abject
or at odds
                    ?
                        (the only justifiable
                        punctuation at this
                        or that
                        point
                        in the assay)

and I wonder now if anybody, if anybody
really doubts, however
moralizing or morally
ambiguous anybody's Milky Way
may be, however didactic
litigious or however little
spare time or
                        (*Ellis Island?* No, that was
                        the year prior—)

and I haven't forgotten about raw participatory concept
neither, nor
Strategic Air Command

I wonder if anybody really doubts
                        (whether this works online
                        or no
                        I wonder)
even today or yesterday or tomorrow or

neither *Night of the Hunter* nor *Marty* and certainly not *Artists and Models*
Jungle Moon Men The Desperate Hours The Left Hand of God Women's Prison (Ida
again) *The Tall Men The Racers The Great Race Bad Day at Black Rock* not *I Am A Camera*
It Came from Beneath the Sea Run for Cover The Man from Laramie The Man Who Loved
Redheads not even *Hell*
on FriscoBay with Edward G(oldenberg) as an
Amato, oh dear

Hi, it's me again.

not *To Catch a Thief* not *Lady and the Tramp Smiles of a Summer Night Battle Cry*
Blackboard Jungle not *Tarantula* not *To Hell and Back* not *Rebel Without a Cause* not
The Seven Year Itch The Far Country Land of the Pharoahs The Man with the Golden Arm
not
Blood Alley not *Ordet* not *Kiss Me Deadly* not *Fire Maidens from Outer Space The Rose*
Tattoo The Night My Number Came Up Oklahoma! Three Stripes in the Sun The Court-
Martial of Billy Mitchell A Man Called Peter The Rains of Ranchipur Mr. Arkadin The
Ladykillers Daddy Long Legs Killer's Kiss

(It came up
I suppose, on that release date.)

I wonder if anybody, anybody any
viewer? really doubts this, what
possibility?
          And the necessity
                         (there's that word
                         again)
self-deceived or otherwise or

Disneyland? Milano? Miles & Trane? Salk? Louis Hartz? *The Petrified Forest*
(on the tube)
and Weldon—

of trying to realize, of trying to
realize it, to realize, what

"I'm altering the vector—
now."

You're way ahead of me.

Satchmo, singing Blitzstein? *French Sonnets*? Parks? hooks? Or Agee? Mingus?
(no picnic, neither)

Did you say Republican
or rhetorician?

no, a public domain
of, what
not dissent alone, no
nor dissertation, but necessary
                              (if disputatious)
relation? Is this, what
the contingency? that
justice
would portend? What a

language. And the greatest good
for the greatest number? I wonder
                              (nor Ike's '55 address
                              to West Point cadets
                              in color
                              to a predominantly white
                              rabbit-eared, and live
                              audience, to the contrary

                              nor Einstein's nor Dean's
                              nor Adelbert Ames, Jr.'s
                              passings, yes
                              nor Narinder Kapany's fiber optics

Can the state use eminent domain
                              (aka Support Our Oops)
to change my domain
name?

& Emmett Till) Sometimes I wonder

This is a terrible mess, no?
if not without its methodology.

Eniac unplugged, Play-Doh, spinout, semper fi, Last Night When We Were Young
end of *the affair*—

Don't Save

Xray

I Need An Agent

with X-ray eyes

                    (*not another
                    software program*)
who can see through
this industry, cut
to the bone, manage
a large advance
someplace in the neighborhood
of my neighborhood.

My neighborhood: chatting about
that restraining order
on your husband
the cop, that clown
is doing absolutely nothing
for my confidence
in your ability
to fit me for a temporary
crown.

Long Live the King!

We had something
living like there's
a war on. IS OVER
if you want it. And when the war
was on, everyone lost
something, some more than
others. I lost my
server, then you, then you
lost me. And apropos
of absolutely nothing
I liked to think my tongue
felt good sliding up
and down the crack
of your ass
while you moaned
out monosyllables. This figures
as they like to say
the body politic, which enjoys it

up the ass. "Fuck me
harder," says the body politic, at once
female and male, despite
my constrained, occasionally
omniscient narration. "And what's wrong
with that?" I say, in clinical apprehension
of being Ettlingered
while licking or, absent the actual
body, clicking.

O love, O wondrous life!

Pardon me, you
snobs. So anyway. Prose is not
out of the question—
I'm a writer
                          (not to put too fine
                          a point on it)

of prose
                          (subtract the line
                          breaks, you'll see
                          kinda)

and from my desk, kids, the new
homestead's mission
control, I can verify
                          (sorta)
that desire continues unabated
                          (these people everywhere
                          walking their dogs
                          holding little plastic bags
                          of shit, clearly)
which has repercussions
for just about everything, for instance
                          (did someone say no ideas
                          but in *poetry*?)
the environment. More people
                          (& more asskissers?
                          this is vital)
with more desire
= more CO_2: the solution
may not be what we wish
for, so be careful
                          (i.e., really really

                                    really
                              smart about)
what you wish for: even a wish
is something
you don't get
for nothing, whoever
you are
or wish to be, Dear Sir.

We may have to reopen
in particular
that fissile case—I think you know
the one
that was dismissed
way back. For the country
despite progresses
                              (note the plural)
has drifted right, left
us a little closer
to the edgy.

I hate to be
like this
                              (i.e., conservatively
                              conservational)
but somebody's
gotta do it, as a conservative
estimate indicates that
our kids' kids will be living
underwater, some of them
if we're not really
really
etc. Sleepin'
wid duh fishes
unless, as some would have it
they have one a them Christian fish
symbols on the ass-ends
of their auto-
mobeels.
                              (*the bible
                              tells me so*)
            So attend
you must
to production
and consumption, writing

and reading and corresponding
materialities, whether pulpy or
translucent mysteries. No side
of such a mapping, however
blurred, can force the issue
without agency, plus
or minus, in all 5-6-7-8
quadrants.

Ahhhhhh-mennnnnn.

> ("I've never understood
> Republicans, the ease
> with which they convert
> their hard-earned cash
> into other people's hard-earned
> morality, and vice
> versa, which, when you think
> about it, has everything to do
> with the discourse of
> mortality and a brined
> pork chop."
>
> Mark Twain, 1888)

This ain't what you call
stock. And I ain't
what you call
a reliable narrator
of internal combustion. Otherwise
you can trust me
so long as you leave behind
your journalistic prejudices.

"When in doubt
leave it out."

"There's nothing I don't know
about knowledge."

"I want enough money, just enough
to go back whenever
someone I've known all my life
becomes an obituary."

"The kids in this bar

could buy and sell me."

Wait—that last
was a mistake. Please delete
when you reedit
for video.

Speaking of which, I am looking for a completed thriller script.
I am looking for a completed comedy script.
I am looking for a completed lesbian script.
I am looking for a completed horror script.
We are looking for a script and a writer

who can muster
the appropriate measure
of obeisance to, to—

And we'll keep looking. Some awful shit happens
to your friends
and you're not around
and suddenly
you're not friends?

Please. OK: No.

No. This is the source
of the schism, my
origin. 'Cause baby when I'm gone, I'm
gone. (Some poets should die
of their reverence
for the abject, their own
awful shit, which they would treat
like Play-Doh. What this translates to
after childhood
is one too many "friends," and a severe shortage
of figs.) Meantime, I need an agent with X-ray eyes who can see through this industry,
cut to the bone, manage a large advance. B/c, to put it mildly, or politely, or analogically,
declining issues have led advances for most of my life, and warm cashews are nowhere to
be found. I'm a writer, so pass me another sheet on the lee side, q.t., down-low, will you?

Gramercy.

Yankee

That's me, yes sir, esp. south
of the Mason-Dixon
or watching Cagney
dancing; or in effect
with a winter storm warning
in effect.

No, the electorate
does not always know
whereof it speaks. Without
exploiting that situation, progressives
need to find a better way to talk
turkey, especially
with turkeys, even
across the aisles.

"They're arguing over
on Poetics again."

Roger that. One should be comfortable
in the woods and out
on the street, keeping
the beat.

(I think there's a tiny man
trapped, screaming
inside my humidifier, out here
in the suburbs.)

((Did you say humidifier
or modifier?))

(((Did you say nose job
or blowjob?)))

((((Think of it: an entire generation
of old ladies
with tattoos above
their sagging asses.))))

Have you been to Billings
Montana?

Neither have I.

Perhaps a moratorium
on travel
is in order. Everyone
who can read
stay home
read a book
about someplace else, i.e., a foreign
habitat.

In my case, the
church.

Or maybe, cook
for yourself.

> ("I wrote and I ate rabbit."
> Viktor Shklovsky, 1922)

A faint whiff of literacy:
I'm in the airport
as I write this
listening to one end
of four cell calls
at once, aging
rapidly

and while tempted
to transcribe
very little of what
I'm hearing
does not say
"love me
and my genes."

But do plunder
Buenos Aires
for their cheap leather goods.

And do
you really intend to visit
Bangkok in that
orange velour pantsuit?
Do they even

have tomatoes
in Bangkok?

>>>READ A BOOK<<<   for christsakes. And then let's talk about
impact evaluation
(this, after all and
strictly speaking
a nonprofit sector).

What I think now
is that, like a book
one world ends
and another begins. How
to do justice
to the certainty of it
the root of it.

(That was a question.)

Brooklyn, Brooklyn
Hail to thee, O Brooklyn—

"Stop marrying
your brother."

"In this course you will learn
how to write captivating
                    (i.e., not un-
                    interesting)
email. Bring a favorite
pen."

Did you say a literary approach to pugilism
or a pugilistic approach to literature?
And what is this "counterculture
blue" I've been hearing
so much about? Or should that be
"counterfactual"? Will
Machinima point the way, or is this
just another high-tech
rumor? You mean there's a light
at the end
of the tunnel
in my wrist? Says
who?

And did you hear what the
Poet Laureate
of Jerkwater declared, that
Jerk?

Just another posh push
poll? Fists, or
fist? Water seeks
its own level, even
jerkwater? You said
you requested a private audience
with the *poet*? And "on a good day"
means, not today?

OK: a $15 buy-in, kids
is not the path
to righteousness

                      (telleth the business manager
                      of the Union).

"RELEASE SEAT BELTS! COME THIS WAY!"

Now you're talking
some sense into me? I see—
I need it. I've got the world
on an abecedarian string, following me
out the door, yep
the door that used to be
a window, out of which prosodic—no
prosaic—no
prosodic condition
seep the (collapsible) conditions
permitting for this Werk

                      (for instance, and for someone like me
                      = hands)

and which are not the sole (negotiable) subject
of this
or any
Werk

                      (to paraphrase
                      something someone
                      or other, could be Ralph
                      Berry, wrote someplace
                      or other, could be
                      Rain Taxi).

Conditions having thus
seeped, and fallen, fallen
and seeped, the door
                    (Door #1)
charting the movement
of spirit to
and fro, requires a step beyond
irony, possibly
out of one's
depths and into a
green acre
or two resembling sheer
probability, the place
or space to be
for those of sound mind and
being of a mind to reform
their minds
                    (i.e., bodies).

"Dream it. Shoot it. Cut it. Live it. Be it."

Talking movies talking
again, on the web. The key word, evidently, is
it. I.e., you're
it, and
it's a hike. And the disembodied voices
from the drive-in speaker
lacked bodies even
before they hit the wire
:   but man, it was *real*.

And not literacy, no. Anything
but. More like following
your nose.

Don't forget
to write, Zsa Zsa. Which
is to say?

Strike it.

Strike it rich.

Zulu

Zulu?

Loved the film as a kid, Stanley
Baker, Michael Caine, Jack
Hawkins and all
at the drive-in, the
Lakeshore
in Liverpool, I believe

                    (shall we fact-check
                    each memory?)

but today
I "see" more, "am"
a better man, have
succeeded
myself, and take note
of the complex-
ions, how they play
off one another.

Haven't I? I mean, succeeded
myself. Who,
me?

Not so, she says. Too trying
and rewarding
to endure, methinks, theethinks, this distance
from one's origins,

                    (the rural-
                    suburban, or vice
                    versa, a short drive
                    from the midsized
                    city, surrounded
                    by small
                    -ish villages, not to say
                    fishing villages)

hence
too ambiguous to assign
definitive value. I've got friends, close
friends, bub, going all the way back
who would be incomprehensible
to my new, heavily armored

                    (i.e., degreed)

friends, and the funny thing is
they know it—a key difference
between my old
and new friends, which latter
know much, live
the examined life, yes, but
haven't been around, some
of them, enough to know what
they're lucky to be
missing out on. And the funny
thing is, my old friends
know this.

Being part Italian
and a Central New York prick
I may be overstating the case, yes
Zeek.

But being part French
and German, or, to be
more specific, Alsatian
and no stranger to verisimilitude
I may not. Mischievous then, sure, a liar
never, or
only to protect you
from the truth.

Either way, "friends" is doing
perhaps too much work
throughout, yes
friends.

Lordy. Well, so: the all-American
alarums and excursions
continue, and @ the services
                              (she was my mother's
                              best friend)
we're, my friends and I, confronted by
"the faith of Christ in black"
face, if you ask me, smartass
blasphemer, if not
critic, if not indefatigable
optimist, at my best, a role
thrust upon me, one might surmise
not unlike those hymns, or that cinnamon item

from Wegman's
the next morning
and entirely unlike that chowderhead, what's his name?
in the White House
who reminds me
of that glazed donut
that somehow made its way
into my pie hole.

(Yum, ugh, chomp. And don't
think there aren't mullahs
I don't like
a lot more, either.)

Really though: what is the proper measure
of one's faith? Me, I must have some
somewhere, here in my back
pocket....

In good faith, any truth
claimed herein
will have everything to do
with the good, Mr. Fish—
and that's the best I
or anyone
can do.

Oh yeah, I might have substituted
for faith
"conviction," but then, why the
hedge, the gift
to Right Wing
Wing Nuts?

Smart Security Saves Time
this on the slip I find
in my luggage after. And a student
I like
writes, in anguish

24. A false hero who presents unfounded claims. (Propp)

Or, the poet accepts the mantle
martyred, and we all feel that much
more blessed, even those of us

who don't know what *cinquecento* means
or have never seen a cinquefoil.

Sad little poet, fighting the good fight! May we
take our leave, sire?
Thank you.

Deep down inside, we *so* want
to poke poetry
in the eye. Blame it on
TV, I suppose, but
I can't. These poetic personae
fluttering about
are just murder

esp. in light of the slaughter
of citizens and soldiers in Iraq
and elsewhere.

Did somebody say *boohoo*?
Did somebody say *intentions*?
Did somebody say *alliteration*?
Did someone say they're sick of *my* identity?
Did someone say they don't believe in exceptional *people*?
Did someone say they'd located an ideologically incorruptible *subject position*?
Did someone say they didn't have a *rhythmic* bone in their body?
Did someone say *Where have all the robots gone?*
Did someone ask to see the centerfold?
Didn't someone say *What the fuck*?

Trying to make a spectacle
out of myself, you   bet, Ziggy
before someone does it for me. To
me? And before
I forget, I wanted to make mention of
"wonderful things"
now and the year of my parents' birth
(1922). Fidelity to fact, of course
is a concern here, as over there
in the history department
but let's not get our shorts
in a knot
over it. And let's recall *now*, in brief
is circa 2006, not 1922 or
1941 or 1967. And man, woman, am I

beat

vegans, Stage Door Canteen, Michael Theune, Ultima Thule, Svengali, Elmer Fudd, Miles Standish, freegans, Capucine, James Caan, Larry David, Grand Panjandrum, Legba, *Alfred Hitchcock Presents*, Lynn Hershman Leeson, silly geese, Black Friday, *Cimex lectularius*, Black Sites, Cyber Monday, Yeshua, Subcomandante Marcos, Peter Viereck, Strawberry Fields, dealers, Aristoxenus, NYU/UAW, the Bismarck, the Seaview, Davy Jones's Locker, the water's edge, *The Last Command,* Davis Schneiderman, the Von Trapp family, Quasimodo, Scheherazade, Riane Eisler, Helen, Ma Tsu, 1348, James Elkins, Saladin, Army Corps of Engineers, Mmorpgs, WNDR, Gino & Carlo's, Budd Boetticher, Bill W., Westport Country Playhouse, Candy Barr, The Persian Gulf, mavens, damsels in distress, knights in shining armor, JT LeRoy, "Binky" Urban, Frances Marion, Ralph H. Baer, Phyllis Diller, Uma Thurman, Lee Miller, Pitcairn Island, hobos, *King Dinosaur*, UFW, complex systems, Roberto Harrison, Christ's creation, Local 320, the Promised Land, the Rust Belt, the business end of the brush, Terangi, Ricardo Cortez Cruz, Garson Kanin, Sylvia Beach, secular humanists, Swearengen, Greensboro 4, Isaac Stern, Fourth Estate, the Sumerians, Gitarzan, happy hunting grounds, 211, Foreign Intelligence Surveillance Act of 1978, Ahura Mazda, bookies, by gum, and we'll soon be old

regardless
of how immature, mature, bad
or good
you may find me. [*Thanks Tom.*—Ed.] Not to nitpick
you Lutherans

>   (from above
>   in the garden)

but what we want
to know is, cryptically speaking
what comes after

>   ///NATION-BUILDING?\\\

We ask without meaning
to come off
as too Eurocentric (like those bodies
that have mattered
and muttered most to us, we suppose)
or aural (we can't
or won't sign, sorry). This business
of the global, poetries
included, promises to be
none too easy
and far too nasty. Has never
been, always
was. Like that sky, recycled
but holding steady
at 90 brightness—try, just try
to touch it.

Let's go public
anyway. That way
at least, one surmises
no one will claim
of us
or our baggage
that we're
too perfect.

As if.

Gotta breathe in & out, gotta
live, you see. And this requires occasional
hacking, reverse
engineering.

>   (see our memoir)

Our old friends

they know this
better than our new friends, or
seem to. Christ
but they seem
to know too much, if you ask
our readers, which latter
will not include
our old friends, or
Henry Wadsworth Longfellow
the 4th, and the majority
of fiscal conservatives.

"Love me"?

"2 + 2 = 0"?

We hope not—yet
                    (i.e., we could all stand
                    to get out more, take
                    a breather, as above)

still we

hope, hoping

someone will call this
a book?

That was a question, ole buddy
ole pal.   Just don't
bet money
on it. Where we come from
this will all be decided
upon, naturally

around someone's, a
friend's, under
let's say, a kitchen
                    (food can kill you
                    like war—no, like that
                    old saying, that good old
                    bad
                    arithmetic, like taking the law
                    into one's own
                    Etc., here, *hear*)

tabletabletabletabletabletabletabletabletabletabletabletabletabletabletable

mesamesames
amesamesame
samesamesam
esamesamesa

I have given you my choices
nor the way, nor the truth, nor the life.

"Do not cast all your cares on Me,
for I no longer care for you."

(cf. 1 Pet 5:7)

4   Turn to your self-cleaning pH electrode.

       Do not let Me be in charge of your life and all that concerns you.

8   Rely on your continuous monitoring level transmitter.

       Do not let go of doubts, anxieties, discouragement.

12   A vibration switch reduces costly downtime on rotating machinery.

       Do not let go of any suggestion that it is up to you alone to figure out every answer to life's questions.

16   Take the guesswork out of temperature measurement with a thermal sensing RTD.

       Do not let go of any thought or feeling that separates you from Me.

20   Everything you need to know about gas detection systems can be summed up in one word.

       Do not let go of fears for the future and do not place everything in My care.

24   Attend the review course entitled "The Essence of Good Chemical Engineering Practice."

       Do not let Me be in charge and be your help in every need.

28   Rent the video "The Why, When and How of Instrument Calibration."

       Do not let My strength be your strength.

32   Join the global network of instrumentation, systems and automation professionals.

        Do not let Me think through your mind.

36   Monitor hydrocarbon contamination in water, even at low levels.

        Do not let Me act through your hands and feet.

40   You have instant access to trained, professional, problem solving representatives.

        Do not let Me speak through your voice.

44   The choice is yours to be yourself.

        Do not rest in the assurance that I am the power and authority of your life.

47.5   Grieve, and be happy. You are the best available.

In the meantime:

"We would like to remind you that Memorial Day is not far off. In an effort to decrease delivery time, we have developed a Computer Aided Drawing system to help our draftsmen in preparing a custom drawing of your memorial...."

17 March 1990

"Narrative is what anybody has to say in any way about anything that can happen has happened will happen in any way."

Gertrude Stein, 1935

& so:

       Yes, baby   have been episodic
couldn't help it, no.
       Blanket statements flawed   engineering
intentions with words the design   (grrrr-aphic & otherwise, surely
       falters BUT
what the hell, there's no business
       like it
       gave it
       a try & now
know-how to begin again
       the next
text, the alterations
       alternatives of
begin & end
       a look at the country
as Stein said, says, might say, a
       heresy, & the double helix, unpaid balances, conception
to execution, make us, mind you, 1
       4-lettered coil.

Just playing around (?)
       transplanting back-
ground, punctuating fore
& aft, microsurgically
       to rediscover
all of this social debris
       piling up
here, at the end
       of all places, a way round
the round mass the
       dank plots the
       whole world treasures.

"Columbus was here"   above a urinal:

       this is definitely NOT Martinique.

            Not America [West], in sum
but no less West-
ern for that. Always had a thing for the hemi, the Amazon, Brazil
one huge chunk
of continental thought, yep. But heck, hey

that's me, & I mean
me, Mister Would-That-I-Had-Owned-More-Muscle-Cars.... *Meanwhile,*

transfers from
        file to file, failing
        all, reformat l+i+f+e
               & light   *e-r-a-s-e the e""v""i""d""e""n""c""e, u|n|d|e|d|i|c|a|t|e|d*
        & sure, $$$ abounds (esp. @ shift 4, har)

the key or clef
        for some har   *dy*
lima,echo,tango,tango,romeo,india,sierra,tango,sierra

                                        GAME OVER

       ~~stricken~~ but the information is   t herein still
chasing me   down, *oui*
       down to no science, *sí*, séance   or performance   maybe
       I be wrong, maybe   I lose the taste   for it
       now
       then, some,times   knowingstill
no place
       to bring it on,   to sit   still   ll   no place,
pointing, panting
       i.e., —> to go, to grow   old   to de   posit
t   rade

       —> like it

                      (i.e., if memory
                      serves)

for our proficiencies, our
devotions

recent and new books from chax press

Bruce Andrews, *Swoon Noir*

David Abel, *Black Valentine*

Paul Naylor, *Arranging Nature*

Kass Fleisher, *Accidental Species*

Tenney Nathanson, *Erased Art* (New West Classics 5)

Heather Nagami, *Hostile*

Caroline Koebel and Kyle Schlesinger, *Berlin Schablone*

Linh Dinh, *American Tatts*

Patrick Pritchett, *Burn: Doxology for Joan of Arc*

Jonathan Brannen, *Deaccessioned Landscapes*

David McAleavey, *Huge Haiku*

Norman Fischer, *Slowly but Dearly*

Keith Wilson, *Transcendental Studies* (New West Classics 4)

Beverly Dahlen, *A-Reading Spicer & 18 Sonnets* (New West Classics 3)

David Bromige, *As in T As in Tether* (New West Classics 2)

Nathaniel Tarn, *The Architextures* (New West Classics 1)

Nick Piombino, *Hegelian Honeymoon*

Jerome Rothenberg, *A Book of Concealments*

Bill Lavender, *While Sleeping*

Elizabeth Treadwell, *Chantry*

Allison Cobb, *Born Two*

Todd Baron, *TV Eye*

Karen Mac Cormack, *Implexures*

Pierre Bettencourt, *Fables*

Heather Thomas, *Resurrection Papers*

Nathaniel Mackey, *Four for Glenn*

Charles Bernstein, *Let's Just Say*

Hank Lazer, *Deathwatch for My Father*

Mark Weiss, *Figures: 32 Poems*

For additional titles please visit our web site: http://www.chax.org/

This and other projects by Chax Press are supported by the Tucson
Pima Arts Council and by the Arizona Commission on the Arts with
funding from the State of Arizona and the National Endowment for
the Arts.

Arizona
Commission
on the Arts

NATIONAL
ENDOWMENT
FOR THE ARTS